Faith and Justification

BOOKS BY G. C. BERKOUWER

MODERN UNCERTAINTY AND CHRISTIAN FAITH

THE TRIUMPH OF GRACE IN THE THEOLOGY OF KARL BARTH

STUDIES IN DOGMATICS SERIES —

THE PROVIDENCE OF GOD

FAITH AND SANCTIFICATION

FAITH AND PERSEVERANCE

THE PERSON OF CHRIST

GENERAL REVELATION

DIVINE ELECTION

MAN: THE IMAGE OF GOD

Studies in Dogmatics

Faith and Justification

BY

G. C. BERKOUWER

PROFESSOR OF SYSTEMATIC THEOLOGY
FREE UNIVERSITY OF AMSTERDAM

Wm. B. Eerdmans Publishing Company
Grand Rapids, Michigan

Translated by Lewis B. Smedes
from the Dutch edition, *Geloof en Rechtvaardiging,*
published by J. H. Kok N.V., Kampen, The Netherlands

ISBN 0-8028-4810-9

PHOTOLITHOPRINTED BY EERDMANS PRINTING COMPANY
GRAND RAPIDS, MICHIGAN, UNITED STATES OF AMERICA

CONTENTS

Relevance

CHAPTER 1

Relevance

THE relationship between faith and justification underscores the relativity of theological science. This relativity, needless to say, is quite another thing than philosophical relativism; it refers simply to the relation of a thing to something other than itself. Theology is relative to the Word of God. This relativity is decisive for the method and significance of theology. It means that theology is occupied in continuous attentive and obedient listening to the Word of God. And since listening, unlike remembering, is always a thing of the present moment, theological questions must have relevance and timeliness. Theology is not a complex system constructed for their own entertainment by scholars in the quiet retreat of their ivory towers. It must have significance for the unquiet times; but it can achieve its proper relevance only in obedient attentiveness, not to the times first of all, but to the Word. The relationship between faith and justification illustrates, if anything can, that theology, being ever relative, must be ever relevant — and is relevant only when duly relative.

It may be true that much of the criticism leveled against theology in the past has been motivated by the same basic unbelief that has always inspired hatred of the dogma and faith of the Church and of the authority of the gospel. This must not, however, be allowed to be used as an alibi for theology wherever it has itself been guilty of provocation. Theologians have not always made it clear that theology is something other than a human speculation carrying its own authority. The word of theology has too often witnessed to itself rather than to the living Word of God. It has too often been articulate without first being attentive. When this has been so, theology has invited reproach — and deserved it.

Theology is often called a systematization of scriptural data. When it is so called, one must immediately ask what is to be understood by *system*. There have been systems which, although begun with a profound research into Revelation, have become arid intellectual theses, whose difference from a theology of the Koran is little more than incidental. If theology is to have meaning for our problematic times, if it is to be a troubler of man's conscience and a comfort to troubled men, then it is more than imperative that our theological reflection be reflection in the Word. Only as a real theology of the Word shall theology avoid the destructive luxury of being a beautiful system with which the instructed few may be entertained, but which stands aloof from the tumult of life. It can and shall have — without any pretensions — living significance for the practice of faith, for the preaching and the confessing of the Church in the modern world.

As we reflect on faith and justification, we shall confront not merely theories, but realities — realities seen and understood only in faith, but, when thus perceived, definitive for our own lives and the life of the Church.

*   *   *

The question of the *ordo salutis* — the way of salvation — has come with peculiar force to the front of contemporary theological discussion. This can be partly explained by three influential factors: the problems raised by the dialectical theology, the renewed discussions between Roman and Reformed theologians, and the so-called Luther renaissance. It may be helpful for a general orientation to consider each of these for a moment.

The dialectical theology has raised acute problems concerning the relation between justification and sanctification, and therewith between faith and justification, problems that had not been seriously entertained for a century. From the very beginning of Barth's theological career these problems formed an important element in his dogmatic and pastoral-ecclesiological program. The current discussions on this point are still defined by the problem formulation of the theological school bearing his name. The dialecticians struck afresh at the heart of all questions — the relation between God and man — and so set the whole field of religious thought in motion. Thurneysen, discussing the drive behind this theological movement, emphasized the radical divine Word of forgiveness and justification which at the time of Barth's early writings seemed to offer the only possibility for life.[1]

The new movement was especially antagonistic to the theological subjectivism of the nineteenth century. This antagonism took its positive form in a search for the truly objective and in an unprecedented attempt to find this objectivity in the divine subjectivity, in the divine initiative of grace, in the word of forgiveness, justification, and reconciliation. Grace was described as "pure objectivity" by Emil Brunner in his *Erlebnis, Erkenntnis und Glaube*, published in 1923. In this book Brunner recalled his readers from all subjectivism and psychologism back to Paul and Luther and their teaching of justification by faith alone. "A judgment over us can be heard, a voice from beyond, transcendent, totally independent of our subjectivity . . . a 'judgment of justification,' an *actus forensis*."[2] Faith, to Brunner, was a "leap," yet the most objective truth. It was a foothold in eternity, an unconditional leap into another world.

Together, Barth, Brunner, and Gogarten waged a *blitzkrieg* against mysticism and intellectualism, pietism and orthodoxy,

---

1. E. Thurneysen, "Zum religiös-sozialen Problem" in *Zwischen der Zeiten*, 1927.
2. E. Brunner, *Erlebnis, Erkenntnis und Glaube*, 1923, p. 98.

moralism and metaphysics, against any attempt to stabilize
the relationship between God and man, against any effort to
secure man against the lightning of God's judgment. Not
mysticism but the Word! Brunner cried to Schleiermacher.
Not man striving for goodness, but man under the free
judgment of God — this was the man that interested the
new theology. It was natural that justification should form
the first center of theological concern, for the new theology
had taken its stand on the Word and the work of God, on
the free act of His mercy. Faith was of interest only in that
it was directed to this free act of God, this incomprehensible
miracle of mercy. Since these first years, the entire way of
salvation has been wrung through the press of theological
dispute, but the basic postulate of God's free act of grace still
defines the discussion.

The question of the *ordo salutis,* the way of salvation, took
a new turn when, in 1930, the differences between Barth and
Brunner began to take on the appearance of real disagreement.
This debate began over the question of the task of dogmatics
and over the so-called *point of contact* in man for God's grace,
but the still unresolved dispute has significance for our present subject also. Brunner found reason to criticize Luther's
famous expression "at once sinner and justified" (*simul pec-
cator et justus*) and insisted, in opposition to Barth, on "the
evidence of the new life."[8] Since then, with variations on
the theme but with the basic strain never really altered, the
discussion has continued *fortissimo.* The old questions about
the way of salvation have taken on the function of a balcony
from which the entire terrain of theological thought is viewed.
And it is remarkable that now — twenty years later — these
questions still prevail in and define the dialectical theology.

---

3. E. Brunner *Vom Werk des Heiligen Geistes,* 1935, p. 57. Cf. also
p. 53: "There is nothing to that which one hears so often these days —
even from those who wish to be Reformation theologians — that while
faith brings new life, the new life remains wholly hidden. This teaching
is neither Reformed nor biblical."

This is an indication of how deeply the *sola fide* doctrine, when it is proclaimed, affects the Church.

A second stimulant to more intense concern with the doctrine of justification is the debate between Roman Catholic and Reformation theology. It is said these days by some Roman theologians that the Reformation *sola fide* no longer suggests an antithesis to Roman dogma, since, now more than ever, it is clear that Rome never intended to devaluate the significance of faith and God's sovereign grace. Indeed, Roman theologians are speaking of the "Catholic" *sola fide, sola gratia*: children are justified and made children of God prior to their having any idea of what has happened to them and absolutely without achievement or merit on their part. This, we are told, is pure grace, as it is also pure grace when a mature person comes to faith. Is it not, then, a grievous misconception to interpret the Roman Catholic teaching as Pelagian?

Every Roman Catholic recognizes profound structural differences between the Reformed and the Roman Catholic Churches. But many are now insisting that the difference does not consist in the one recognizing and the other denying sovereign grace. The Council of Trent confessed grace as the "first factor" of the way of salvation, and this is no less than any reformer has done. The differences touch only the manner in which this grace relates itself to the sinner and to the means which grace uses to achieve her purpose.

No Reformed theologian will deny what Trent said. It is indeed true that in Romanism grace is the starting point of the way of salvation. But the differences arise as soon as the next stop is approached. The conflict opens around the doctrine of infused grace and that of imputation. It is waged around the nature of the divine justification and its relation to the entire course of life. In short, the relation between sovereign grace and the merits of good works still forms a wall of disagreement between Rome and the Reformation churches.

Perhaps, it may be said, the Catholics have a point. Perhaps the lines are not drawn now as they were in the sixteenth century. Perhaps much misunderstanding can be cleared away by admitting that the Catholics, too, honor the priority of divine grace. Perhaps we are now in a position to recognize a real religious accord which centuries of theological bickering have concealed. Perhaps, as the Roman Catholic theologians now say, the doctrine of meritorious good works, which scandalized Luther, does not efface the glory of grace, but actually, in its deepest intent, honors it.

Were Luther and Calvin only shadow boxing? Or did they, in their strike against Roman work meritoriousness and indulgences, really hit an essential weakness of the entire dogmatic structure? The heart of the matter is open here. Ought we to return to Rome? Or must we continue to pray for her conversion? Must the conflict continue, or is it merely over differences in the logical grouping of the various elements of the *ordo salutis* in which, at bottom, both sides mean the same thing and therefore ought to come to agreement? Questions like these, newly arisen, have naturally impelled us all to reflect further on faith and justification.

The revival of interest in Luther, which has reached the point of a Luther-renaissance, has also added to the contemporary relevance of the doctrine of justification. The new studies of Luther's preaching are not motivated by purely historical interest. There is a marked desire to get a clear insight into the basic religious principles and motivations of the Reformation. This is not to say, of course, that the nineteenth century had forgotten Luther completely. One need recall only the Lutheran Erlanger School, with Frank and von Hofmann, which sought support for Schleiermacher's theology of religious experience in the sixteenth century Lutheran confessions. The Ritschlian theologians also had a great deal of interest in Luther. Nevertheless, no earnest and responsible study of Luther was made then. The traditional notions of the difference between Lutheran and Reformed theology had been established — the one being typified as religious and the other as more speculative.[4]

In our century, new life was brought to Luther studies by Karl Holl,[5] who was aided immeasurably by the discovery of Luther's lectures on Romans given in 1515 and 1516. One of Holl's first conclusions drawn from these and other documents was that Luther taught an "analytic" justification. This shattered the comfortably established opinion of Ernst Troeltsch that Luther's teaching was a mere "re-modeling" of medieval thought, that it formed an "essential unity with the basic characteristics of ancient and medieval thought."[6]

Though the distinction between analytic and synthetic justification was not new with Holl (it had often been used in Ritschlian circles), it was now given a new edge. Synthetic justification was understood as a declarative judgment of God whereby the sinner was justified solely on the basis of the work of Christ. It was this that Holl understood Luther to reject and which Holl himself rejected. Melancthon, said Holl, made the great mistake of narrowing justification to a mere declaration that man was righteous, while Luther understood justification as a real transformation of man as sinner to man as righteous. When God justifies the sinner, said Holl, He does more than make a synthetic judgment, a forensic declaration. He literally makes man righteous. If God were to declare a man righteous who is really unrighteous, God would be dishonest: God cannot seriously call black white, nor an unrighteous man righteous. Justification would then be a fiction, a treating of man *as though* he were righteous — an idea which Holl called the fatal "as though." Such a justification, he says, is more an external imputation than the power of renewal.

---

4. As, for instance, was irresponsibly done by M. Schneckenburger, *Vergleichende Darstellung des lutherischen und reformierten Lehrbegriffs,* 1855.
5. K. Holl, *Luther,* 1917.
6. E. Troeltsch, *Die Bedeutung des Protestantismus für die Entstehung der modernen Welt,* 1928, pp. 32 f.

Holl described God's justification of man as an *analytical*, by which he meant that God's judgment is based on what man in reality is or shall certainly become. Justification, thus, is eschatologically considered. "God's declaration of justification is determined by the soul which He has in view; this declaration proposes a decision, an act of divine volition, the ground of which is the divinely intended sanctification of man."[7]   Hence, the phrase *analytical justification*. God's justification of man is at bottom an analysis of the renewed man.   Holl saw this description of justification as providing the only real point of contact between justification and sanctification, and the only means by which the divine integrity could be maintained.   Man's own righteousness is the reason for God's declaring him so.   If this righteousness is not present and cannot be foreseen as present, justification deteriorates into a doctrine of fictitious imputation.

At this point, the revived interest in Luther joined the current dogmatic controversy.   For Barth entered the discussion here with a blast against Holl's reading of Luther. If Barth had to choose between Roman Catholicism and Holl's interpretation of Luther, he would choose Rome.   Barth was not alone in his attack on Holl.   In fact, the question of analytic or synthetic justification became the central issue in the entire controversy about the sovereignty of God's grace.

Meanwhile an old work on Luther was rediscovered, a work which in its own time went largely unnoticed.   It was a study by Theodosius Harnack written in 1862 and reissued in 1927 in the conviction that it "was of great, perhaps definitive, importance for the modern understanding of Luther."[8] Harnack accented the doctrine of imputative justification as well as the reality of divine wrath in Luther's theology, and the revival of his study provided a rallying point for opposi-

---

7. Holl, *Luther*, p. 124.
8. W. F. Schmidt in the forward to T. Harnack, *Luthers Theologie mit besonderer Beziehung auf seine Versöhnungs- und Erlösungslehre*, I, 1862, and II, 1885, reissued, 1927.

tion to Holl. Holl was a disciple of Ritschl and was undoubtedly influenced accordingly in his interpretation of Luther. The dialectical theologians by and large leaned heavily on T. Harnack.

Through these three factors, then — the rise of dialectical theology, the renewed conflict with Rome, and the revived study of Luther — the doctrine of justification has been set in the center of theological interest.

Holl spoke for many when he said that justification "is not a doctrine that has had its day; it is the *eternal gospel.*" Even those who read the gospel differently than Holl does felt the same about the importance of justification. The confession of divine justification touches man's life at its heart, at the point of its relationship to God. It defines the preaching of the Church, the existence and progress of the life of faith, the root of human security, and man's perspective of the future.

Theological subjectivism did not err because it stressed too heavily the living relationship of divine truth to human faith. This relation is so essential that theological reflection dare not for a moment turn it into an abstraction. If theological reflection loses sight of this vital relationship, it becomes sterilized, turns into an intellectual orthodoxy, and loses all contact with the people of God. The mistake of subjectivism was rather this, that it subjectivized the *norm* of God's revelation in Jesus Christ. It gave the human subject a determinative, creative function and made revelation dependent upon the subjective creation. Schleiermacher defined Christian dogma as an "expression of the Christian pious disposition as construed by the reason."[9] His theology and the ravages of the modern era resulting from it reveal the illegitimacy of its conception.

The fruits of this subjectivism must not, however, close our eyes to the unique relation that does exist between faith and revelation. The doctrine of justification cannot be grasped

---

9. F. Schleiermacher, *Der Christliche Glaube,* 1884, 6th. ed., p. 94.

apart from it. It is not as though justification flows from
two springs, God's declaration and man's faith. It is faith
that recognizes and accepts the exclusiveness of God's salvation. As we shall see, this correlation between human faith
and divine justification forms the pivot of our study.

* * *

Dogmatic reflection has no power to produce faith, regardless of how keenly it may analyze the Holy Scriptures. It,
like every believing enterprise, is totally dependent on faith.
It lacks all semblance of autocracy. It makes no claim to
self-sufficiency. It has no authority over the Church; it can
only humbly serve the members and servants of the Church
by searching out and describing the various interrelationships
in the Word and so to stand guard over the wealth of God's
grace, turning back every subtelty of human pride which
would gladly swallow the golden coin. And one of the
principle entrances to the treasury of grace is the doctrine
of justification. The way of salvation from sanctification to
perseverance has often been lost because theology went wrong
at the point of justification. The conflict between Rome and
the Reformation in the sixteenth century began at this point,
but it spread through the doctrines of sanctification,
perseverance, and assurance of salvation. This suggests the
indissoluble bond between the problems of faith and justification, faith and sanctification, and faith and perseverance.
This is what makes justification such an existential problem;
it is really the heart of the matter.

* * *

Is it possible for us, then, to strip the problem of all
historical barnacles and, beginning afresh, unburdened by
tradition, to address ourselves to the Bible? What is the relation of fresh Scripture study to the history of dogma and the

confessions? Every theological work manifests throughout
the dependence of the writer upon a miriad of others. Take
only the comparatively recent line of theologians: à Marck,
van Mastricht, Turretinus, Schleiermacher, Ebrard, Philippi,
Frank, Bavinck, Kuyper, Elert, Koepp, Strange, Barth, and
Brunner — not one of them is wholly independent of those
who came before him. No one can slough off the questions
that have grown up in theological history and confessional
development.

There is a living interaction between immediate theological
reflection on one hand and the defined dogma of the Church
and the entire line of dogmatic history on the other. The
relationships — both thetic and antithetic — are evident in
the various confessions, though they were intended simply to
confess anew the divine truth. Each was meant as a proclamation of the gospel, in a sense a timeless reflection of perpetually relevant and comforting truth. This intention gives
the confessions of the Church their living continuity. Yet,
each confession is also a product of a historical situation. The
Heidelberg Catechism mirrors the controversy with the
Lutherans, the Canons of Dort are defined by the struggle
with the Remonstrants, the Belgic Confession reflects opposition to the anabaptists, the Helvetic Confession of 1562 is
clearly directed against Rome, the Westminster Confession of
1647 opposed the Catholic mass; and so it is with every confession. The Church that most keenly wishes to subject itself to the gospel never frees itself from historical definition.
This is no concession to historical relativism. The Bible itself
is historically conditioned.

Dogmatic study, like confessional expression, wears the
image of its day. It can never be lifted above the problems
of its environment. Bavinck, for example, witnesses in every
chapter to the questions of the nineteenth century. We meet
there shades of Schleiermacher, Ritschl, Julius and Theodore
Kaftan, Frank, and Ihmels. Now, however, the situation is
changed, and dogmatic reflection has taken a new turn. This

does not mean that contemporary problems are totally other
than those of the nineteenth century. Many of the questions
that occupied the attention of nineteenth century theologians
have been passed along to us. The questions of the relationship between revelation and history, the virgin birth, and the
physical resurrection are our legacies from the past century.

Nevertheless, coincident with the turn of the century,
a change of key occurred in theology — in almost every locus
of it — as in many other sciences. To mention just one
example — the problem of eschatology as it is handled by
Heim, Althaus, Barth, and Cullman is quite other than it was
when discussed by Ritschl and Hermann. With the different
approach of the twentieth century new problems have arisen:
the relation between creation and Christ, the doctrine of the
image of God, and the confession of the two natures of Christ,
for example. All these reflect the "changing of the times."
There may be difference of opinion as to the significance of
the change, but that a theological page has been turned is most
evident.

The contemporary theologian faces an intensely fascinating
array of dogmatic problems. He works against the background of a time in which the very meaning of human existence is in question. The danger, of course, is that contemporary theology be determined in essence by the crisis of modern
life. In fact, this very danger itself forms an important part
of the theological discussion today. Even while the dialectical
theologians were still of one mind the question was raised
among them as to whether Barth's theology was concerned
really with the judgment of God or with the modern crisis
consciousness. The further development of Barth's doctrine
of grace has taken the edge off this question, but the danger
that theology should become only a reflection of its times
remains very actual. It is, however, impossible even in theology for one to remove himself from the time in which he
lives. We cannot work in a vacuum, even as we cannot
jump into the maelstrom of relativism. With the gospel as

our guide we must set our feet in the center of troubles. In theology irrelevance is as fatal as relativism.

A strange mingling of voices is heard in the discussion that shall occupy us in this volume. We meet Kohlbrugge and Kuyper, Böhl, Osiander and Newman, Barth and Brunner, and Luther and Calvin. We hear them all and ask what they say about the crisis of humanity and the crisis of human certainties. And it is all relevant to the way of salvation. But, though we hear the sound of many voices, we hope always to have our ear to the Word. The purity and clarity, as well as the relevance, of our study will depend on our attentiveness to the Word of revelation. The absolute pre-eminence of the Word of God above all human explications provides our only perspective. Willing captives of the Word, we shall try to keep in mind what Paul says about total obedience: ". . . (for the weapons of our warfare are not of the flesh, but mighty before God to the casting down of strongholds); casting down imaginations, and every high thing that is exalted against the knowledge of God, and bringing every thought into captivity to the obedience of Christ" (II Cor. 10:4, 5).

Such obedience will bring with it a sharp distinction between theological study and speculation. It will alert us to the danger of leaving theology to consort with speculation. For speculation, or imagination, as Paul calls it, emasculates theology, trades confession for system, and makes the theologian forget the incomprehensibility of God. He who is tempted to cross beyond mystery through the depth or breadth of his own thought, may well recall another statement of Paul: "Knowledge puffeth up, but love edifieth" (I Cor. 8:1). This is no judgment against knowledge as such, of course. Yet, even when Paul is speaking of worthy knowledge, he adds, "We know in part."

Paul's humbling reminder applies to theology no less than to any other study. Theology can only bow before mystery.

And this applies perhaps particularly to the relationship between faith and justification. We are not to address ourselves
to a logical synthesis that we can frame in a finished proposition, thus ending the matter. We shall be dealing with the
living relation of man to God the Father of Jesus Christ. Even
with this, however, we have not passed out of the danger zone.
We shall be in temptation on every page. The history of the
Church and her theology warns us perpetually: "Let him
that thinketh he standeth, take heed lest he fall" (I Cor. 10:12).

We proceed, then, in fear and trembling, yet with a
measured confidence and joy.

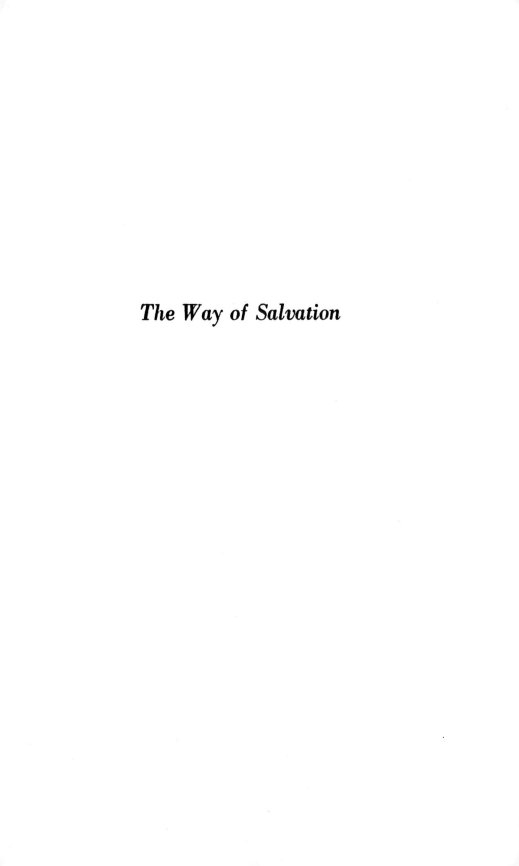

The Way of Salvation

CHAPTER II

The Way of Salvation

THE *way of salvation* — or the *ordo salutis* — is actually the application to man of the salvation which was won for him by Christ in His three-fold office of prophet, priest, and king. Theologians have had a lot of trouble with the word *application*. For one thing it has been criticized as dividing up salvation into objective and subjective sides — the divine and the human — with each placed mechanically opposite the other. It has also been pointed out that the notion of a *way of salvation* was first developed in the eighteenth century, the era of dogmatic decadence and scholasticism. The development of the *ordo salutis* was allegedly part of a growing systematization of theology, of a speculative and rationalistic tendency. It was evidence of too much concern with the regenerated or believing man in the various stadia of his life and not enough interest in the riches of the objective divine salvation.

The Reformation was said to have talked more simply and more scripturally when it merely put the *way of salvation* within the focus of the single correlation of grace and faith. "Salvation was attributed" by the reformers "to the free grace of God and its believing acceptance. Thus, only grace and faith were considered under the *ordo salutis*."[1] Luther wanted nothing other than this, yet he gave stimulus to the later development when, in his smaller catechism, he said that

---

1. Kalweit, "Heilsordnung," in *Religion im Geschichte und Gegenwart*, II.

the Holy Ghost *calls, illumines,* and *sanctifies* through the gospel.[2]

Such statements as these are said later to have led to a more systematic concern with the human soul in the process of being saved. This in turn tended toward a schematization of salvation, which Otto Ritschl called "a symptom of decadence." It was traceable presumably to an erroneous tendency within the Reformation to think first of God as the Giver and Dispenser of salvation and secondly of man as believing, thence to put more accent on the *order* of salvation than on the salvation itself.

The criticism of the *way of salvation* was motivated by a fear that the subjective life of faith be made an independent area of study. This would mean that we had lost the objectivity of divine salvation and placed divine justification as a mere phase or step within the process of salvation. It was further said that the theological over-attentiveness to the *way* of salvation meant that salvation was thought of as human activity, and that the basic Reformation acknowledgement of salvation as grounded exclusively in God's grace was therewith abandoned.

If this be true, then the entire *ordo salutis* formulation should immediately be rejected. It appears to us, however, that the critics of the *ordo salutis* often fail to see that the motive behind it was the maintenance of the sovereignty of God's grace. The origin of the *ordo salutis* was closely connected with a virulent defense of the gospel. It was not merely a hyper-anxiety about the pious, regenerated man that stimulated the various constructions of the *way of salvation.* The analysis of the application of salvation to man was part of a criticism of those who underestimated the influences of sin

---

2. "I believe that through my reason or strength I cannot believe in Jesus Christ, nor come to Him, unless the Holy Ghost calls me through the gospel, illumines me through His gifts, sanctifies and preserves me in true faith." *Die Bekenntnisschriften der evangelisch-lutherischen Kirche,* ed. J. T. Müller, 1928, 12th ed., p. 358.

on the human soul and who minimized the perversion of human nature. We cannot deny that the *order* often prevailed over the *salvation*, nor that theologians often forgot that analysis and organization of theological material had significance only if they helped to make clearer the message and reality of salvation. Though it may satisfy an appetite for logical construction, the order of salvation can be given no independent significance. If it is given any independence, the most highly developed and neatly systematized *ordo salutis* will lose all connection with Christian piety and will lend credence and assistance to the devaluation of dogma and dogmatics.

It has been pointed out that there is a profound difference between sixteenth century theology and later theology in their manners of speaking about the way of salvation. The development of Lutheran theology after the Reformation era has been burdened with the charge of making the scheme of salvation an end in itself. We may add that Reformed theology has not always perceived and shunned this tendency. This is manifest in the too familiar practice of placing justification and sanctification on one level with faith, conversion, and good works in the *ordo salutis*. The intent of this practice is undoubtedly to show the indissoluble relationship which each of these elements sustains to all the others, that is, to emphasize the unity of the *way of salvation*. In spite of this respectable purpose, the simple biblical perspective of the *way of salvation* is often lost in the practice. This also helps to account for the endless variations in the *ordo salutis* that appear in the history of Reformed theology.

The theological schematization of the order of salvation, thus, has no significance by itself. The order is relevant only in that it aids us to appreciate the fullness of divine salvation. It does not include the entire course on which man walks in the way of salvation. The ways along which God leads man to His salvation are so richly varied that it is impossible to

circumscribe them all in fixed stadia. When theology defines
the *ordo salutis*, it is to "display the treasures of salvation and
blessing which God in Christ has earned for His people and
which He in the Holy Spirit apportions to them." It is, further, "to suggest the benefits that the one great work of
redemption brings."[3] Our reflection on the *ordo salutis*
concerns, finally, what Calvin expressed simply as "the manner
in which the grace of Christ is obtained, the fruits that come
to us therefrom, and the works that follow."

The simplicity with which Calvin describes the way of
salvation is rather striking. His attention never moves from
God's salvation to the believing man. It is only through the
Holy Spirit, he emphasizes, that the promise of salvation
penetrates our hearts.[4] The Holy Spirit may be viewed as
the key which opens to us the treasures of the kingdom of
heaven. Calvin, immediately after saying this, begins his
exposition of faith; but he is concerned only with the faith
"whose stability is wholly in Christ."[5] Faith has a stable
basis — the gracious promise. And faith "never stands
firmly till it comes to the gratuitous promise."[6] This attitude
toward faith, as worked in us by the Holy Spirit, controls
Calvin's entire treatment of the way of salvation. Not until
he has discussed and disposed of many errors which corrupt
the sovereign character of grace does Calvin begin with the
subject of the Christian life. Calvin's whole work on this
subject continually circles about one point — salvation in
Christ. Thus, when he gives separate treatment to justification by faith, after discussing faith, repentance, and regeneration, it is not as though he therewith begins a new subject.
He is quite conscious of his concentric mode of thought,
describing justification as the main pillar on which religion

3. H. Bavinck, *Gereformeerde Dogmatiek*, III, 1928, 4th ed., p. 596.
4. Cf. Calvin, *Institutes*, III, i, 4.
5. *Ibid.*, III, ii, 1.
6. *Ibid.*, III, ii, 30.

rests.[7] Here, too, Calvin's primary concern is the correlation between faith and justification. Only after having set this relation in the light of Scripture, does he address himself to the subjects of Christian liberty, prayer, and election.

It would be unreasonable to criticize Calvin's method as being unsystematic. Though one does not find an *ordo salutis* in Calvin, in the sense of its later development, there is nonetheless an order, perhaps better called an orderliness, which is determined by salvation in Christ. Salvation in Christ — this is the center from which the lines are drawn to every point of the *way of salvation*. The lines themselves may be called faith. They connect every step on the way of salvation to salvation in Christ. Thus seen, the relation between the *way of salvation* and Christ's salvation will keep us from placing the objective and subjective elements of salvation opposite each other as a duality. The character of faith resolves all tension between objectivity and subjectivity. For faith has significance only in its orientation to its object — the grace of God. Thus, *sola fide*, instead of directing our attention to the believer, points us away from him to grace and God. We may apply this as a touchstone to every consideration of the *ordo salutis*: all lines of the life of faith must meet at the center, the grace of God.

* * *

Abraham Kuyper once noted a difference between older and newer terminology in the subject of faith and grace. The Belgic Confession uses the older terminology in Article 24, where we read: "We believe that this true faith, being wrought in man by the hearing of the Word of God and the operation of the Holy Spirit, regenerates him and makes him a new man, causing him to live a new life, and freeing him from the bondage of sin." The relation between faith and regeneration as found here is suggestive of Calvin's statement "that we are regenerated by faith."[8] The newer terminology is that used

7. *Ibid.*, III, xi, 1.
8. *Ibid.*, III, iii.

by later theologians, who limit regeneration in the *ordo salutis* to the *beginning* of the new life.[9]   Kuyper spoke of the older Reformation and confessional terminology as the result of an "unfinished conception," of which the later, more limited, idea of regeneration was "the consistent development."[10] Kuyper approved this development, but not simply out of love for system.   The refinement of terminology resulted, according to him, from a desire to protect the Reformed concept from misconception.

Nevertheless, we cannot share Kuyper's attitude toward the words of the confession. Kuyper said that later theologians abandoned "this more or less questionable manner of speech and set regeneration more in the foreground."   He went on to say that the confession contained a "subjective conception." Here Kuyper's criticism of the confession suggests, I think, that he puts too much importance on the arrangement of the steps in the *ordo salutis*.   The decisive point is the way in which faith is related to God's grace.   And this was in the confession, as it was in Calvin, above reproach.   It is just as unreasonable to brand the formulation which we find in Calvin and the confession as subjective conceptions as it is to charge post-confessional development with shifting interest from grace to man.   Faith involves a certain subjectivity, but a subjectivity which has meaning only as it is bound to the gospel.

This is precisely the marvel of the work of the Holy Ghost — that He is the origin of this faith.   It is not the order as such that is decisive.   It is how one understands God's salvation that determines whether sovereign divine grace is properly respected.   To make a system of a certain *order* of salvation does not insure purity of doctrine.   Nor does simplifying the *ordo salutis* guarantee a pure confession of grace.

---

9. Cf. H. Bavinck, *Gereformeerde Dogmatiek*, IV, pp. 28ff.
10. A. Kuyper, *Het werk van den Heiligen Geest*, 1927, 2nd ed., p. 381.

This becomes more interesting and important when we see that it is not possible to deduce a fixed *ordo* from the words of Scripture and their order. An *ordo* is often read from Romans 8:30: "And whom he foreordained, them he also called: and whom he called, them he also justified: and whom he justified, them he also glorified." Other texts are also used in this regard. Consider I Corinthians 1:30: "But of him are ye in Christ Jesus, who was made unto us wisdom from God, and righteousness and sanctification, and redemption"; I Corinthians 6:11: "And such were some of you: but ye were washed, but ye were sanctified, but ye were justified in the name of the Lord Jesus Christ, and in the Spirit of our God"; and Titus 3:5: "Not by works done in righteousness, which we did ourselves, but according to his mercy he saved us, through the washing of regeneration and renewing of the Holy Spirit." The great variety which is apparent in the words Paul uses brings to mind the expression of Seeberg: "Only the richness, not the order, of the way of grace comes to expression."[11] The text which looks most as though it presents a definite sequence is Romans 8:30, in which Paul, while discussing election, notes the phases of the *way of salvation* — calling, justification, glorification. Sanctification is conspicuously absent in this list; and anyone with a mind to accept Paul's list as a systematic arrangement of the course of salvation, would surely be unwilling to omit sanctification from the sequence.

What does Paul intend here? He evidently means to characterize salvation in Christ, the salvation which arises from the depths of the Father's heart and reaches out into time with an eternal blessing. The context suggests that Paul does not have a sequence in mind. He is talking about the work, and particularly the prayer, of the Holy Ghost (Rom. 8:23, 26, 27), about hope (Rom. 8:24, 25), about love to God (Rom.

---

11. R. Seeberg, "Heilsordnung" in *Protestantische Real-enzyklopädie*, Vol. 7, p. 596.

8:28), and about the cooperation of all things for the good
of those who love Him (Rom. 8:28). A simple biblicism,
which sees a sequence here, would bring us into trouble when
faced with I Corinthians 6:11, which puts sanctification before
justification.

It is clear that we cannot answer the question of the *ordo
salutis* with a combination of scriptural terms. The determinative question is whether, in the *way of salvation,* we give sufficient expression to the fact that the life of the believer —
from first to last — is embraced by divine salvation.

We need not be afraid that by reflecting on the relation of
this divine salvation to human subjectivity we are harboring
an objection to the sovereignty of grace. Salvation has everything to do with human life down to its most subjective facets.
Neither need we think that the way of salvation has to do with
an "application" of salvation, as though a "second salvation"
— a subjective one in distinction from the objective work of
Christ — had to be realized. Rather, it is concerned with the
achievement of the purpose of grace. When a person sees
this clearly, he will never make faith one distinct point in the
way of salvation. To do such a thing with faith, says
Stephen, "Robs it of its fundamental and comprehensive significance as the one unifying doctrine of evangelical Christianity."[12] If the *ordo salutis* were really intended to be
a straight line drawn through a sequence of causal factors it
would be open to the same objections that we have against
the Roman Catholic concept of the function of faith as a pre-
paratory phase preceding justification or infused grace.
Reformation theology has always protested that faith thus
loses its central and total character and becomes a mere step
on the way of salvation. In contrast to this devaluation of
faith, the Reformation confessed *sola fide,* meaning thereby
to emphasize the universal significance of faith. In this way
faith possesses no unique functional value; it rests wholly in

12. Horst Stephan, *Glaubenslehre,* 1928, p. 88.

God's grace. Theological study of the *way of salvation,* or
ordo salutis, must, then, always revolve about the correlation
between faith and justification. It must simply cut away
everything which blocks its perspective of this *sola fide.* Heresy
always invades the *ordo salutis* at this point, and this is why
it is so necessary to realize that the entire *way of salvation* is
only meant to illuminate *sola fide* and *sola gratia.* For only
thus can it be confessed that *Christ is the way.*

*   *   *

Theologians, in their studies on the *ordo salutis,* have often
done injustice to Christ by making subtle distinctions and
divisions between the objectivity and subjectivity of salvation.
Christology, for instance, has often been reckoned with the
objective while soteriology has been put in the subjective
sphere. Salvation was thus practically construed as composed
of two factors, one divine and one human, while the totality
of salvation was to be seen in their combination. Grace and
redemption were considered as the objective state of affairs.
Grace and freedom of choice, grace and merit were part of
human activity. But in this way the *correlation* between
faith and justification was lost sight of. A tension arose
between the work of God in Christ and the role of man.

The Church has to be perpetually alert to this sort of
division of the work of salvation into two cooperating parts.
The spectors of Pelagianism, semi-Pelagianism, synergism,
humanism, Arminianism, and even Roman Catholic dogma
remind us of how the salvation, the *salus,* can actually be ob-
scured by a systematic *ordo salutis.* That such notions of
cooperation could have been so often proclaimed within the
Church as self-evident truths is possible precisely because
the salvation of the Lord does indeed pervade man's whole
existence and is not in the least a reality which remains foreign to man's concrete experience. The gospel does not come
cooly to inform man of a new objective state of affairs. It

invades man's life as a call to belief and conversion, to love and obedience. It is so pointedly directed to the concrete existence of man that we may speak of an essential correlation between faith and salvation. The salvation of the Lord does not fall on the world as rain upon an arid countryside. It creates a personal relation in which this salvation is experienced and known in love and thankfulness.

Nevertheless, this intimate correlation occasioned many heresies in the Church. And these heresies were often germinated when men began to put a peculiar emphasis on the *way*, the *order* of salvation, the way of faith and conversion, of penance and repentance. When this has once begun, it becomes increasingly difficult to appreciate Christ's "I am the Way." It became increasingly difficult to understand that every analysis of the *way of salvation* should only emphasize and clarify this confession. To walk in the way of salvation can only mean to live in and through Him.

The doctrine of salvation tended toward error even in the early years of the Church's life. The believer's conviction that he was walking in the way of salvation was inverted and became the idea that faith, conversion, and penitence were achievements. This began a tendency which moved away from the essential biblical presentation and led, in the Middle Ages, to a hopeless obscuration of salvation. The *way of salvation* was given a certain independent value whose significance all further systematization and ordering could only increase. It was not forthrightly denied that Christ was the way, but the confession of Him as the only *way of salvation* was unable to flower in its natural vitality. To give one example of the tendency of the early Church in this respect, we may mention the *Didache*. The *Didache* described two ways, the way to life and the way to death. The way to life was defined: "First, thou shalt love God, who made thee, and second, thou shalt love thy neighbor as thyself."[13] The way to death was defined as being "evil and full of cursing, murder,

13. *Didache*, Chap. I.

adultery . . ." and only at the very end of the long list of characterizations comes "lacking in fear of the Lord."[14] This is quite different from describing the way to death simply as the way which is other than *the Way*. Following the *Didache* one could consider himself safely off the way to death while hardly wondering at all whether he were in the Way which is Christ.

It is striking how often and with what stress the Scriptures discuss being "on the way."   Paul, for instance, says that he serves God after the Way, which some "call a sect" (Acts 24:14).   Christ spoke of a narrow and a broad way (Matt. 7:13, 14), while the messengers of the Pharisees and Herodians said to Him in irony that He taught the "way of God" (Mark 12:14).   The idea of the way was so concrete in the minds of the apostles that Peter could speak of blaspheming the "way of God" (II Pet. 2:2), of "forsaking the right way" and "following the way of Balaam" (II Pet. 2:15).   It is clear that *the way* for the apostles is defined in both its beginning and its process by the salvation given in Christ, that is, by Christ *the Way*.   Christ, recall, answered Thomas's question, "How do we know the way?" by pointing to Himself (John 14:6).

The New Testament use of the word *way* has been interpreted as a contrast to the contemporary mystical "way" to immortality.   In any case, it is clear that the New Testament does not consider the way as a long struggle toward a certain goal, immortality in this instance, but, primarily, as Christ. And it pictures *walking on the way* as the knowledge that one is in Christ who is the Way.   This is the same way of salvation on which the Old Testament believers also walked. It is the way of peace, on which, according to Zechariah's prophecy, our feet are guided by the tender mercy of God (Luke 1:78, 79). Paul described his life and conduct as "my way in Christ, even as I teach everywhere in the Church"

---

14. *Didache*, Chap. V,

(I Cor. 4:17). It is the way of righteousness (II Pet. 2:21) as opposed to the way of Cain (Jude 11). It is the right way (II Pet. 2:15), the way of the Lord (Acts 18:25, 26; cf. also Rom. 11:33 and Rev. 15:3).

This simple and obvious presentation of the concept *way* in Scripture is not open to the charge of biblicism, as contrasted with a serious theological attempt to understand the *ordo salutis*. The scriptural view of the *way* on which God brings us must be determinative for all explication of the theological presentation of the way of salvation. Both Church and theology present examples of how quickly the scriptural motif can be left behind. How often have not nomism and antinomianism abandoned this way, sometimes hardly noticed! Sometimes generations of Christians have lost the joy of the gospel by having gone amiss on the *way of salvation*. This is why it is perpetually necessary for the Church to reflect on the *ordo salutis,* or, as we think better to say on the *way of salvation.* The purpose of her reflection is not to refine and praise the logical systematization. It is to cut off every way in which Christ is not confessed exclusively as *the Way.* This defines the character of the entire doctrine of soteriology. The Church seeks therein the fulfillment of Christ's promise concerning the coming of the Holy Ghost, who, He said, would "guide you into all truth," that is, He shall point the way into all truth. ". . . He shall not speak from Himself. . . . He shall glorify me: for He shall take of mine, and shall declare it unto you" (John 16:13). When we speak about faith and justification, we shall try only to make clear the correlation between them and to show that in this correlation the way of the active religious man is not a way side by side with Christ, *the* Way, but that faith becomes true Christian faith only *in* Him. We shall have to emphasize that faith knows only one Way and one certainty in that Way: "I have set Jehovah always before me: Because He is at my right hand, I shall not be moved" (Ps. 16:8).

Confessional Reconnaissance

CHAPTER III

Confessional Reconnaissance

As WE turn to our main subject, we are conscious of entering a field on which theologians have engaged each other in dispute almost perpetually since the early days of the Church. The struggles with Pelagianism and semi-Pelagianism, with Rome and the Remonstrants are all concerned with the relation between faith and justification. Strange, though, that so much hostility should be kindled at this point. Surely here we could expect, at least amongst those who accept the authority of Scripture over their thought and confession, a universal and profound accord. For the Scriptures speak about justification through faith with the utmost clarity: "Being therefore justified by faith, we have peace with God through our Lord Jesus Christ" (Rom. 5:1). And again, "We reckon therefore that a man is justified by faith apart from the works of the law" (Rom. 3:28).

Further reflection, however, suggests that even where the phrase *justified by faith* is not rejected in so many words, it has been given interpretations which were sure to be contested. An example of this is the attitude of the Roman Church toward *sola fide* and *sola gratia*. The Roman Church, claims one of its theologians, accepts both of these as unreservedly as did Paul and the reformers.[1] Such a claim prods us on to a more careful study of the relationship between faith and justification as understood in various quarters, especially since Roman Catholic theologians today are insisting with

---

1. W. H. van der Pol, *Het Christelijk dilemma*, 1948, p. 75 (English translation: *The Christian Dilemma*, 1952).

more than usual persistency that the religious motive of the Reformation is fully honored by the Roman Church. This, they say, is the gratifying part of the drama of the great schism. Of course, they recognize differences; the Roman view is often presented as somewhat more complicated, while that of Protestantism is set up as the product of oversimplification. But, at any rate, it is suggested that Rome and the Reformation had more in common than both realized.

Given this situation, it will be most useful if we begin by surveying the fields where the struggle over *sola fide* has, for the most part, been waged. We shall address ourselves, to this end, to a few of the confessions of the churches of the Reformation. Needless to say, this does not mean that the confessions are absolutely decisive. They themselves arise from the conviction that we can and may speak only as we put ourselves under the yoke of Scripture. Our reflection, too, and for the same reason, must proceed in the train of Scripture. But we can hardly circumvent that bitterest of all struggles for a pure understanding of the gospel, the Reformation of the sixteenth century. It was then as at no other time that justification through faith was trumpeted as the article with which the Church stands or falls. *Sola fide* was not presented as a discrete aspect or section of the confession. It embraced the whole gospel. And this conviction is reflected in a number of Reformed and Lutheran confessions.

* * *

The Heidelberg Catechism, after it has presented the Apostles Creed, asks what the *profit* of all this really is. It had already turned this keen, practical edge to each of the various individual articles: Christ's holy conception and birth (Q. 36), His sacrifice (Q. 43), His resurrection (Q. 45) and ascension (Q. 49), and the glorification of our Head, the Christ (Q. 51). It asked, furthermore, about the *comfort* of the doctrine of the resurrection of the body (Q. 57) and

Christ's return (Q. 52). In concrete fashion, thus, the significance to the believer of God's mystery of salvation in Jesus Christ was brought to the foreground.

Finally, in Lord's Day 23, the question is put: "But what does it profit you now that you *believe all this?*" The answer, which is related to the whole of faith and its content, is: "That I am righteous in Christ before God, and an heir to eternal life." Faith has intense relevance to this "profit," this benefit with which the Catechism is so warmly concerned. Faith is not a reasonable acceptance of certain truths, after which it can be set aside for the immediate practical affairs of the day. Through faith man participates in reality, a comforting reality, to be sure, and in a perspective of an eternal future.

The phrase *in Christ* is included in the declaration of personal justification. We are, as it were, conducted into a court of law to hear a merciful declaration of pardon. But the answer displays to us the unique character of this declaration. The accusation was not without grounds; it was secured by incontrovertible facts. The offense that had to be judged was the reality of great sin against God. And this was not something brought up out of a hazy past; the accused is still set for a plunge into the worst of evil. This is all so irrefutable that the sinner can do nothing but admit the justness of the charge.

There would seem to be no possibility of acquittal. But there is an unparalleled counterbalance to the reality of guilt. Christ Jesus is confessed: He has satisfied; He makes good the righteousness, justice, and holiness; and He is the cause of the pardon. He is the surprise of God's unexpected salvation from the just accusation that still is being brought against us. The impossible has here become undoubted reality. The result is an electrifying and truly incomparable judgment of pardon. The doors swing open; the soft lights of the new freedom are shed over our whole future — we are heirs of eternal life.

It is in this connection that faith is mentioned, qualified by the word *alone*: justification is through faith alone. We are now miles away from a cooperation between divine salvation and the human work of faith. For this faith is directed exclusively to Christ, in the recognition that His righteousness and His acts alone could create the amazing situation in which a man can say: ". . . God, without any merit of mine, of mere grace, grants and imputes to me the perfect satisfaction, righteousness, and holiness of Christ, as if I had never had nor committed any sin, and myself had accomplished all the obedience which Christ has rendered for me" (Lord's Day 23). Notice the phrase *as if*. It suggests, perhaps, that we are being told of a fiction, an illusion, a pretence. It recalls the so-called "As if" philosophy of Hans Vaihinger, who tried to demonstrate the great significance of the fictitious for the various sciences.

But this "as if" of the Catechism has to do with far more than a fiction. There is, indeed, an element of analogy, for we have not in reality performed this obedience. We have certainly sinned and are certainly sinners. We were in fact disobedient and slaves of sin. But the creative force of Christ's righteousness is so good and so tender and so miraculous that the new situation can be sketched in terms like the Catechism's "as if." The reality of our performance is not commensurate with the "as if" of the Catechism, and yet we are faced with the immeasurable blessing of Christ's work which is valid for eternity at God's judgment seat. Jesus Christ is the secret of the "as if."

He is its content. Therefore it is an accurate formulation of the message of divine justification. It finds its counterpart in Scripture: "Come now, and let us reason together, saith Jehovah: though your sins be as scarlet, they shall be white as snow; though they be red like crimson, they shall be as wool" (Is. 1:18). "I, even I, am he that blotteth out thy transgressions for mine own sake; and I will not remember thy sins" (Is. 43:25). "I have blotted out, as a thick cloud, thy transgressions, and, as a cloud, thy sins: return unto me; for I have redeemed thee" (Is. 44:22). "Who is a God like unto thee, that pardoneth iniquity, and passeth over the transgression of the remnant of his heritage? he retaineth not his anger for ever, because he delighteth in lovingkindness. He will again have compassion upon us; he will tread our iniquities under foot; and thou wilt cast all their sins into the depths of the sea" (Mic. 7:18, 19).

There is a striking commentary on the *quasi* of Lord's Day 23 in Zechariah 3, where Joshua the highpriest, with Satan at his right hand, stands before the face of the angel of the Lord. Joshua, accused by Satan, wears a filthy robe, yet the accuser is turned away. "And Jehovah said unto Satan, Jehovah rebuke thee, O Satan; salem rebuke thee: is not this a brand plucked out of the fire?" (Zech. 3:2). But there is a difference in Lord's Day 23; here the accuser is not Satan but our own conscience. The "as if" for this reason gets a unique color; it stands in bold relief against the drabness of our own stained conscience and confessed guilt.

Everything is really said in an unobtrusive phrase, *in Christ*. The possibility and reality of justification are concentrated in this one phrase. This appears most clearly in the manner in which faith is approached. It is not added as a second, independent ingredient which makes its own contribution to justification in Christ. On the contrary, faith does nothing but accept, or come to rest in the sovereignty of His benefit. Further, to ward off any misunderstanding, Lord's Day 23 declares with a touch of emphasis, that we are not acceptable to God because of the worthiness of our faith. Grace is exclusively and totally God's; therefore, says the Catechism, we can do nothing else but accept it through faith (Q. 61). To walk the way of faith is simply to admit that Christ is the Way. These are the accents of the Reformation. Every conceivable fancy of merit in any human quality, position, or

activity which might have been viewed as a cooperating cause
of our justification before God is excluded. *Sola fide* and
sola gratia: it is plain that they mean the same thing.

Christ is the one light that burns here. Faith sees nothing
except in this Light. And this is the miracle of faith as the
gift of God.

*　*　*

Though justification through faith gets special attention in
Lord's Day 23, the same faith-reality is described elsewhere
in the Catechism. This is most striking in Lord's Day 22
where the forgiveness of sins is discussed in terms similar to
those used in the description of justification by faith —
satisfaction made by Christ, the gift of Christ's righteousness,
the escape from God's judgment in spite of the sinful condition
against which we are engaged in a life-long struggle. In
other connections, too, we catch glimpses of the richness of
salvation: payment for our sins, redemption from the lordship
of Satan, and the assurance of eternal life (Q. 1); the in-
grafting through faith and by mere grace of all God's benefits
(Q. 20); the reception of the Savior with a true faith (Q.30);
membership in Christ through faith (Q. 32); becoming a
possession of Christ (Q. 1, 34); the covering of our sins before God's face (Q. 36); participation through faith in Christ
and all His benefits (Q. 53); implanting in Christ through
true faith (Q. 64); confidence in the forgiveness of sins
(Q. 81); acceptance of the promise of the gospel with a true
faith (Q. 84) without merit on our part and merely out of
grace (Q. 86). These are pillars of the Christian faith; together they form a collonade about the correlation between
faith and salvation.

The Belgic Confession draws the same lines. Jesus Christ
is the point from which all rays extend. This is especially
apparent in Articles 22 and 23. Faith is not a second factor
in justification, we are told. It plays its role in justification
by embracing Christ and all His merits, seeking nothing out-

side of Him. Referring to Romans 3:28, the Confession says: "Therefore we justly say with Paul, that *we are justified by faith alone, or by faith apart from works*" (Art. 22). This is particularly striking since the confessors knew quite well that the phrase *justified by faith alone* appears nowhere in Paul. They had been reminded of this time and again by Rome. Exegetical or grammatical error is improbable. Their formulation was determined by the conviction that, along with the way of the law, all ways other than faith ran to dead ends. Through this fact the only way, the way of faith, became the more clear. *Sola fide,* as it is used in this passage, is completely identified with the Pauline doctrine that salvation is "apart from the works of the law." This is to be understood, as it is in Lord's Day 23, as meaning that faith is not an independent meritorious act accepted by God as good enough for Him. It is a total commitment to the one Way, Christ. Really, it is not faith itself that justifies; faith is only an instrument with which we embrace Christ, who is our justification.

We shall have to return to the idea of faith as an instrument somewhat later. But even here the intent of the term is clear — the radical amputation of all prestige from faith. Faith is not a human act that complements God's act of grace. Not according to the Belgic Confession. Faith holds us in fellowship with Him who is our justification. And His merits "which have become ours, are more than sufficient to acquit us of our sins" (Art. 22). This is the theme of the psalm which the Church's theology has on its lips. Our justification lies in free forgiveness (Art. 23). The obedience of the crucified Christ — this is the *alpha* and *omega* of our justification. He covers our disobedience with His obedience, our unrighteousness with His righteousness. He gives us courage, frees us from the torments of a guilty conscience, dissolves our dread of standing alone before God. The justified man need not be like Adam when confronted by God. His courage takes the place of Adam's terror. It is the "as if"

of the Catechism that changes things so radically. And this
"as if" agrees with Article 23 of the Belgic Confession:
"And, verily, if we should appear before God, relying on ourselves or on any other creature, though ever so little, we
should, alas! be consumed. And therefore everyone must
pray with David: O Jehovah, enter not into judgment with
thy servant; for in thy sight no living man is righteous" — a
remarkable and meaningful conclusion to an article on justification through faith alone.

*   *   *

Although the Canons of Dort do not speak very extensively
about justification by faith, in what they do say it is clear
that Christ is the total substance of our justification. This
is the relation between faith and salvation in Christ taught by
Dort: "But such as receive it and embrace Jesus as Savior
by a true and living faith are by Him delivered from the
wrath of God and from destruction, and have the gift of
eternal life conferred upon them" (I, 4). We hear again
the same theme that we heard in the Catechism and the Belgic
Confession: pure grace, Christ as the foundation of our
salvation (I, 7). Salvation is, of course, viewed in the light
of election. That election occurs on the basis of foreseen
faith or of the obedience of faith is repudiated (I, 9): to say
that faith is a condition of salvation is an "injurious error"
(I, Rejection of errors 3). Such an error renders impotent
the pleasure of God and the merits of Christ, and through it
"men are drawn away by useless questions from the truth
of gracious justification and from the simplicity of Scripture"
(ibid.). Election is the fountain of all saving good (I, 9).
Believers are given over to Christ, gifted with true faith,
justified, and made holy. Salvation comes forth from unmerited election (I, 17). The Canons' sharp protest against
the Remonstrants demonstrates how the priority of grace is
firmly grasped, and how the confessors were in no spirit for

concessions. They were unable to be conciliated by the Arminian concession that the foreseen faith on the basis of which we are justified was a gift of grace, nor by the statement that God "chose out of all possible conditions (among which are also the works of the law), or out of the whole order of things, the act of faith which from its very nature is undeserving and which offers only incomplete obedience, as a condition of salvation" (I, Rejection of Errors 3). This was unacceptable precisely because it made faith a condition, chosen from all possible conditions, actually putting faith and the law on the same level, though one is accepted by God and the other not.

The Canons are not remarkable for subtlety. They simply permeate themselves with the all-sufficiency of the Savior. For this reason humility and confession of guilt characterize much of them. As much as grace is praised, so much is the worth and merit of human work abjured. This is what was missing in the Remonstrant thesis that election waited on foreseen faith, conversion, sanctification, and godliness, so that the complete and decisive election was reserved for the man who is "more worth than he who is not chosen." The Scripture knows of no such comparative worthiness, as the fathers of Dort realized, quoting Paul: "But if it is by grace, it is no more of works" (Rom. 11:6).

A single theme plays through all three documents, the Belgic Confession, the Heidelberg Catechism, and the Canons of Dort — the theme of *sola fide*. And this is the heart of the Reformed confession. The various and varied expressions are religiously simple and transparent. The fathers understood that justification through faith alone was the confession pre-eminent, the confession *sine qua non*.

* * *

Was there a common Reformation confession on this important point; were the Lutheran and Calvinistic Reformation

united in this profound confession of divine grace?   It has
been said more than once that there was not only a confessional
and dogmatic divergence, but a deep religious cleavage between the two.   Schneckenburger,. in his comparative study
of the Calvinistic and Lutheran movements, saw a radical
difference, not only in Christology and sacraments, but in
the doctrine of justification as well.[2]   The Lutheran construction of the doctrine was alleged to have been more sharp in
its antithesis with Rome.   The Lutheran doctrine was more
"synthetic," the Reformed more "analytical," with the *sola
fide-sola gratia* getting much more play in the Lutheran than
in the Reformed confession.[8]   Schneckenberg's argument has
not, however, stood the test of comparative readings in the
two confessional groups.   His error arose mostly from reading into the Reformed confessions the arguments of certain
later Reformed theologians.   A brief excursion into a few
Lutheran confessions will reveal that Schneckenberger's thesis
holds no water, that in the crucial points there is a profound
correspondence between the Reformed confessions as we have
already seen them and the Lutheran ones.

We may note first the Augsburg Confession, in which the
Reformed conviction on justification is very lucidly expressed.
The idea of merit is wholly disowned, as is the possibility of
facing God with one's own powers, merits, or good works
(Art. IV).   In the articles in which the new obedience, faith,
and good works are discussed in defence against the charge
that good works were prohibited by the Lutheran doctrine,
the necessity of good works is stated in such a way as to
insist that we do them, but not that we may be justified
by the doing of them (Arts. XX and VI).   The Augsburg
Confession polemicizes against Rome's doctrine of free will
and the ability to please God apart from grace and the help
and work of the Holy Spirit.   Rome, we read, says less than

---

2. M. Schneckenburger, *Vergleichende Darstellung des lutherischen und
reformierten Lehrbegriffs*, 1855, 2 vols.
3. *Ibid.*, II, p. 31.

formerly about alms, pilgrimages, fasting, etc. (Art. XX), and now proclaims the necessity of faith, "on which in previous times she was practically silent." She says now that a man is not justified by works alone, but that he is justified by faith and works. The Augsburg Confession rejects this new construction just as finally as it did the former one.

He who considers himself able to earn redemption in one way or another denies Christ and seeks a way of salvation that is condemned by the gospel (Art. XX). *Sola fide* is proclaimed in place of all doctrines of works (Art. IV). God imputes righteousness to this faith (Art. IV). If we have done everything, we are still unprofitable servants. In all this, the confession is conscious of proposing no new doctrine, but only of translating the gospel. Thus, it cites Ambrose as saying that he who believes in Christ is saved, not through works, but only through faith apart from merits (Art. VI).

The background of this confession is the Pauline message, along with the words of Christ about the unprofitable servants and His insistence that "Without me, ye can do nothing" (Art. XX). We read of the imputation of righteousness in Romans 3 and 4 (Art. IV), of the relation of the natural man to the Spirit of God in I Corinthians 2:14, of the only Mediator in I Timothy 2:5, of faith as the gift of God in Ephesians 2:8, and of justification through faith in Romans 5:1 (Art. XVIII). This doctrine is a message of reassurance and comfort to the conscience terrorized by its inability to come to rest through its works. The Augsburg Confession is so convinced that it only translates the gospel, that it considers any charge of heresy against itself a violation of Christian love and unity.

Sola fide comes again into prominence in the second part of the Confession, the section dealing with various abuses. For instance, in the article on distinctions in foods it is said that when man must earn grace through such human institutions the doctrine of grace and faith is maligned — regardless of how pre-eminently faith is held above other works.

Recalling Paul's struggle against human traditions, the Confession teaches that "we are not made holy by our works, but rather through faith in Christ alone, a doctrine that has almost disappeared."

This theme, then, is the same in Lutheran and Reformed confessions, and displays the existence of a profound Reformation unity. Calvin's agreement with the Augsburg Confession underscores this early concord.[4]

*   *   *

What has been said of the Augsburg Confession holds no less for the Apology for the Confessio Augustana, in which a defense is made against fierce Roman criticism.[5] The doctrine of justification through faith alone is indicated as the highest and most important article of the faith, and as the key to all the doors of Scripture.[6] The critics are accused of a total ignorance of what faith, grace, and righteousness mean. They have robbed human consciences of the treasure of the knowledge of Christ, and it is therefore the more necessary to establish the doctrine of justification in the Apology.[7]

The teaching of justification in the Apology has been the subject of a good many debates since the appearance of the

---

4. Calvin's attitude toward the Augsburg Confession proves how keenly Calvin appreciated the religious depth of the Lutheran Reformation. Cf. the famous statement of Calvin, before his meeting with Luther: "Though he call me a devil, I shall honor him as one of the foremost of God's servants" (cf. K. Holl *Calvinstudien,* pp. 79, 115). Holl writes that the Lutheran doctrine of justification forms the heart of Calvin's *Institutes* (*ibid.,* p. 116). He calls Calvin "a Lutheran from the very beginning" and says that Calvin was always conscious of being "heir to Luther." This is indeed true as far as the doctrine of justification is concerned. Luther, before Calvin, preached from the rooftops the sovereign grace of God. If certain specifically Calvinistic doctrines are mentioned in opposition to this, let it be remembered that everything doctrinally specific has its right to existence only if it is a pure translation of the gospel.

5. References to the Apology are from J. T. Müller, *Bekenntnisschriften der evangelisch-lutherischen Kirche,* 12th ed., 1928.

6. Müller, p. 87.

7. *Ibid.*

document, debates which arise from differences in interpretation of certain articles. The discussions have to do with the relation of this confession to the teaching of Luther himself. The most important question was whether in writing the Apology Melanchthon did not introduce a new view of justification. It is claimed that this new element was the cause of later erroneous developments concerning the forensic character of justification.[8] Melanchthon, not Luther, is said to have become the molder of popular opinion on the doctrine. The forensic or declarative emphasis in Melanchthon is distinguished from the more ethical construal of Luther. It was especially in his contention with Osiander, it is said, that Melanchthon moved away from Luther. Here he began to wrap the relation between justification and sanctification in a blanket of fog, up out of which the later discussions about analytical and synthetic justification were to loom.

These discussions have been, until the present day,[9] generally unfruitful, in our opinion, a misfortune occasioned in part by the tendency to take the terms of the Apology as fixed scientific phraseology. It is encouraging, therefore, that later Lutheran theologians, such as Elert, have emphasized the religious character of forensic justification as it is perceived in Luther as well as in the Apology.[10] In the Apology, as appears convincingly from a close study, there was no devaluation of the renewal of man (which is usually discussed side by side with justification). There was, however, an earnest attempt to dig into divine grace, the deepest ground of justification.

We are criticized, says the Apology, because we teach that the believer receives forgiveness of sins through Christ only

8. Cf. K. Holl, *Die Rechtfertigungslehre im Licht der Geschichte des Protestantismus,* III, 1928, pp. 525 ff.

9. The debate is focused particularly on Art. 72, and then especially on the words: *ex iniustos justos effici seu regenerari* and *justos pronuntiari seu reputari.* Cf. J. Kunze, *Die Rechtfertigungslehre in der Apologie,* 1908; H. Bavinck, *Gereformeerde Dogmatik,* IV.

10. W. Elert, *Der Christliche Glaube,* 1940.

by faith, apart from any subjective merit.[11]   The Apology
delivers the countercharge that the critics have put Christ in
darkness, have buried Him anew, so that we cannot recognize
Him any longer as the only Mediator.   For they deny that we
receive forgiveness of our sins from Him only through grace
and without merit, and dream that we are able to merit forgiveness through good works and obedience to the law.[12]
They do not understand how sinful our heart is, and do not
know that we forget all merit and all work when our heart
feels the wrath of God or when our conscience is full of
dread.[13]   The devotion of the Apology is to the radical Pauline
antithesis between justification through faith and the righteousness of works.[14]

This becomes the more clear in the section on justifying
faith.   The uniqueness of this faith is, of various ways, the
most discernible in its gravitation toward its object and content.   Faith is the kind of divine service that is poured out
and given to me, in contrast to that in which I do the libations.
The promise is received through faith; all worthiness and
merit are disclaimed, and grace and mercy receive all the
praise — for grace is received without merit.[15]

A remarkable parallel with Lord's Day 23 of the Heidelberg Catechism occurs here: faith does not justify as though
it were in itself a noble work; it justifies only in that through
it the promise of grace is accepted.[16]   Reject *sola fide*, and
you must tear pages from Paul's testimony, the Apology re-
minds us, including such as read that we are saved by grace
through faith, and that not of ourselves, for it is the gift of
God; "not of works, that no man should glory."[17]   Herein is
the exclusiveness of grace confessed.   *Sola fide* is not an

---

11. Müller, *op. cit.*, p. 87.
12. *Ibid.*, p. 90.
13. *Ibid.*
14. *Ibid.*, p. 94.
15. *Ibid.*, p. 96.
16. *Ibid.*
17. *Ibid.*, p. 100.

exclusive hobby that prohibits recognition of other truths. It does not exclude evangelization and the sacrament; it excludes only our own merits. At this point there is an extensive explanation of why we are saved through faith and not through love or good works. Love and works are not disqualified; love must follow faith. However, we are not to build our confidence on love, as though for its sake and through it we should expect to receive forgiveness of sins and redemption from God.[18]

Love is distinguished from faith, for *sola fide* points to the divine-transcendent character of redemption in Christ, to *His* work and *His* love as the only grounds for our salvation. This explains the keen-edged protest against Rome's devaluation of faith to a preparation for justification, to an intellectual assent, to a thing yet to take its form from love and good works. Faith gets a more central position in the Reformation than it can possibly have in the Roman Catholic faith; it is a total commitment to God's mercy which encounters us in Christ.

He who seeks to understand *sola fide*, writes Melanchthon elsewhere, must realize that "we have only divine mercy, and not human merit, to thank for our justification."[19] In the same treatise, he follows his discussion of justification with the claim that the activity of faith, the works of faith, are to be understood in Paul's sense, that faith works through love. Melanchthon does not sever the bond of faith and love, not even in reaction to Rome's appeal to Galatians 5:6. But within the activity of faith, the critical, evangelical function of *sola fide* remains perfectly intact.

* * *

From this all but complete review of the Confession and the Apology we have been able to catch an inkling of the force

---

18. *Ibid.*, p. 108.
19. P. Melanchthon, *Grundbegriffe der Glaubenslehre* (Loci communes), F. Schad edition, 1931, p. 162.

of the Reformation antithesis between faith and works. We can follow the same lines in other Lutheran confessions, in the Smalkald Articles and Luther's Catechism, until, at last, the Lutheran doctrine of justification is given its final formulation in the Formula of Concord. Again in this larger document faith is sketched as an instrument and means "whereby we lay hold on Christ the Savior, and so in Christ lay hold on that righteousness which is able to stand before the judgment of God."[20]   The terminology of the Formula of Concord is more fixed and rigid than that of the Apology, and differences of interpretation are hardly possible. Justification is taught as being a pardon for sins[21] in order to maintain the forensic character of the doctrine. The more precise formulation does not bring about a lesser appreciation for moral renovation and good works, but it does fix the relation between justification and sanctification. It refutes "that faith bestows salvation upon us for the reason that that renewal which consists in love towards God and our neighbor, commences in us through faith."[22]   Justification and sanctification are cleanly distinguished; and justification is described as a divine judgment upon the sinner.[23]   Faith corresponds to this justification; it accepts this divine judgment of grace, and therewith it disavows all meritorial claims.

Sola fide!

This brief confessional review will have given the wrong impression if it suggests that all subsequent development of the doctrine of justification has continued to translate the gospel with similar faithfulness. In Melanchthon's *Loci* of 1559 there is a perceptible shift from the original confession: the Word of God, the Holy Spirit, and the non-resistant human will are now set side by side. Enough to remind us

---

20. Müller, *op. cit.,* p. 528. Translation from Schaff, *The Creeds of Christendom,* 1877, III, p. 116.
21. *Ibid.,* p. 529.
22. *Ibid.,* p. 530 (Schaff, *The Creeds of Christendom,* III, p. 120).
23. *Ibid.,* p. 613.

that *sola fide* is not a sort of trade-mark which guarantees the purity of scriptural thought! On the other hand, it is quite untrue to say that the tendency toward a forensic or juridical justification during the period leading up to the Formula of Concord was an about-face from Luther's more ethical teaching.[24] The forensic justification of the Formula of Concord is not a slip into the net of a scholastic, intellectual order of salvation; it is the end result of a desire to keep the *sola fide* and keep it pure. Elert has said quite correctly that forensic justification implicitly held an antithesis to the scholastic idea of justification, and that declarative justification was only another facet of the righteousness of faith.[25] This was the uniting truth of the sixteenth century. All differences, some of which were not unimportant, within the Reformation stood in the shadow of this transcending verity.

For this reason, too, it is impossible to characterize the Lutheran and Calvinistic confessions as being respectively anthropocentric and theocentric. This dilemma has bothered us too long, as has that other false antithesis — soteriological and theological. If we say that the Lutheran confessions underline the comfort of justification to the restless conscience, and then interpret that as a tendency toward anthropocentricism, we have missed the real point of the confessions. We should be doing the same thing as is done when the allegedly more theological Belgic Confession is contrasted with the Heidelberg Catechism in which "my only comfort" is the ruling motif. The Catechism is then supposedly soteriological and the Belgic Confession theological, with the implicit suggestion that *soteriological* is the same as *anthropocentric*. This is also implied in the irresponsible oversimplification which says that the Lutheran Reformation is characterized by its *sola fide* and the Calvinistic by its *Soli Deo Gloria*. This is, in the light of Scripture, a completely false antithesis. We

---

24. W. Elert, *Morphologie des Luthertums*, 1931, I, p. 88.
25. *Ibid.*, p. 93.

must get at the meaning and intent of *sola fide* and *Soli Deo Gloria*. The Lutheran *sola fide* is essentially directed to the glory of God in His mercy and grace, just as it is in the Calvinistic confessions, and the Calvinistic *Soli Deo Gloria* is not and ought never to be abstracted from this same mercy and grace. Out of their essential contexts the phrases become irreligious bromides.

Paul thought he was giving glory to God by persecuting the Church (cf. also John 6:2). The phrase *Soli Deo Gloria* was, as it were, emblazoned across the life and work of Ignatius Loyola, founder of the Jesuits. In his *Exercitia spiritualia* he says repeatedly that man is created to praise God, to honor Him always and serve Him only. It was not for nothing that Loyola was said to have been obsessed with obedience. Nothing, says Loyola, may motivate man nor guide him other than the service and praise of God; man must be a staff in the divine hands. It is hardly surprising that the Jesuits honored humility as the noblest of all virtues. This should warn us against making *Soli Deo Gloria* an abstract, fine phrase, a neat and formal measure of judgment. In contrast, *sola fide* and *Soli Deo Gloria* were significantly united in the life of Abraham. They were, indeed, one. "He wavered not through unbelief, but waxed strong through faith, giving glory to God" (Rom. 4:20).

In faith God is honored. This is why the Catechism is indeed soteriological, but not anthropocentric. For between the comfort of *sola fide* and the objectivity of *Soli Deo Gloria* there is a beautiful correspondence. They belong together.

The Reformed confession of *sola fide* is a warning sign along the path of Church history. The phrase carries no guarantee against the deceits of the human heart. No formula is a security for the glory of God. *Sola fide* makes sense only in the act of true faith. But the confessions of the Reformation are plain. They tell of grace without the works of the law; they witness against the glory, the elevation, and the trustworthiness of man. They whisper of the comfort of God's redemption, but in such a way as to suggest the danger of making man's comfort the *alpha* and *omega* of Christianity. The warning is needed, for we would undoubtedly enjoy making of the doctrine of justification a projection of our own wishes and desires, a postulate of our own distress. But *sola fide* points the other way, toward God's elective love in Jesus Christ who takes priority over all human desires. This is why *sola fide* is theocentric, and *therefore* soteriological. For the grace of God *that bringeth salvation* has appeared to all men (Titus 2:11). This description of grace concludes with the expectation of the *glorious* appearance of our *great God* and Savior Jesus Christ (Titus 2:13).

Sola fide!
Soli Deo Gloria!

The Reformation and the Holy Scriptures

CHAPTER IV

The Reformation and the Holy Scriptures

THE confessions of the Reformation are impressive for their persistent appeal to the Holy Scriptures. This is pre-eminently true of their statements on justification. The framers of the confessions were evidently moved by a conscious, moment to moment desire to let the Scriptures themselves speak. One senses that they did not try to frame a new doctrine or a new form of Christianity, but merely wished to fall back on and listen to the old gospel. No matter how little the letters of Paul influenced pre-Reformation theology, the reformers did not establish, in reaction, a specifically Pauline gospel. The freshness of much Reformation terminology — really only Pauline terminology revived — did not at all mean that the reformers had eyes only for Paul. The reformers read hard and long in the entire Scriptures. Luther, for example, though he appeals much to Paul, was convinced that the doctrine of justification by faith was taught clearly and extensively in many other places in Scripture. We need only be reminded of his readings in the Psalms, his views on the letter to the Hebrews, and his intense interest in the Gospel of John and many other portions of Scripture.[1] Melanchthon, too, in his *Loci* cites an impressive number of examples from Old Testament history, the Gospels, Peter, Acts, and Hebrews — besides Paul's irrefutable witness to the scriptural character of the evangelical faith.

---

1. e.g. Genesis, cf. E. Seeberg, *Studien zu Luthers Genesisvorlesung,* 1932, pp. 80ff. Cf. also Luther's frequent appeal to the Psalms in his exposition of Romans.

It is, then, quite untrue to say, as is often done, that the reformers made a preferred selection of Scripture passages, while avoiding others; just as it is untrue that they appealed only to Paul. The common Roman Catholic malediction that Paulinism was "Luther's heresy" is a misrepresentation of the Reformation, to say nothing of its implicit slur on the harmony of Scripture.

It is undeniable, of course, that Paul's letters played a peculiarly significant role in the Reformation. In reading the sermons of the Reformation era one almost hears the voice of St. Paul. Reformation preaching was, in a special sense, Pauline preaching. And with this we touch upon a matter of immediate relevance to our subject. We have already mentioned the common charge that the Reformation was one-sidedly Pauline and that it thereby mistook the part for the whole of the gospel. Furthermore, it is sometimes charged, the Reformation did not even make use of the complete Paul; it limited itself almost exclusively to the witness of Romans and Galatians. If this is true, the inheritance of the Reformation is rather an inherited impoverishment than a rich legacy; it has left us a distortion, a one-sided interpretation of the gospel, instead of a restoration of the whole.

This accusation against the Reformation is not *a priori* nonsense. We cannot shrug off the ubiquitous danger that a theological distortion of the gospel be supported by isolated extractions from Paul. Take Marcion as an example. While the Church's theology was still maturing, Marcion appealed to Paul as the only apostle to have preached the pure gospel. This gospel, accordingly, was to be sifted from the Jewish-Christian interpolations and be made the critical norm for the further development of Church teaching. This assertion was accompanied, of course, with an unscrupulous mutilation of the sources. Nevertheless, Marcion is proof enough that one can work one-sidedly with Paul and deduce from him fantastic theological schemes quite untrue to the mind of Scripture. Marcion was clearly guilty of violent and biased selection; but even with honest intent one can distort the unity of Holy Scripture by extravagant and one-sided appeals to certain portions of Scripture. The danger of this is ever acute. Spiritual crises in the history of the Church have often occasioned renewed appeals to Paul: Augustine, Luther, Valdez, Kohlbrugge, and, currently, Barth, each in his turn leaned heavily on Paul. Is it *a priori* impossible that in the tension of the struggle against Rome the reformers were partial and fragmentary in spite of their copious use of Paul? In that case, would Reformed-Paulinism be any more valid than Johannine Christianity, for example, or Sermon on the Mount Christianity?

Peter is the apostle of Rome, runs the saw; Paul is the apostle of Luther. With this, it is often said that the figure of Peter soon superseded that of Paul in the early Church; not the disciple whom Jesus loved, nor Paul, of whose life we know the most, but Peter, is the apostle whose influence has been the greatest. One of the alleged reasons given for this is that Paul, in thinking through the implications of the gospel, reached a depth to which the Church could not follow. His prophetic conception of the fundamental contradiction of flesh to spirit and of law to grace never awakened popular support, but, rather, aroused opposition. It is quite possible, we are told, that Peter was embraced as a mediating figure between Hebrew Christianity and Gentile Christianity, and, in general, between justification by works and justification by faith. It is not accidental, then, that Peter should be the apostle of Rome and Paul the apostle of Luther.[2] This type of argument suggests again that the Reformation might have

---

2. This argument was put forth recently by J. L. Klink, *Het Petrustype in het Nieuwe Testament en de oud-Christelijke letterkunde*, 1947, p. 153.

been one-sided.   Could this be why we ordinarily associate
Paul rather than Peter or John with the Reformation?

It is surely true that the Roman Catholic Church and
theology have grown rather cool to Paul's gospel.   But the
polite aloofness between Roman Catholicism and Paul can
hardly be explained by a lack of popular response to Paul's
teaching.   The weakening of the antithesis between law and
gospel at St. Peter's was occasioned rather by an irreligious
emasculation of the gospel of sovereign grace.   The history
of this nomistic vitiation of the gospel illustrates how truly
Paul spoke when he said that the gospel is not according to
man and therefore provokes the resistance of "another gospel"
(Gal. 1:11, 16).   This explains why Paul was driven to the
background of theological thought until the Reformation
began to understand him anew.   Not only the theologians,
however, but thousands of simple believers as well recaptured
the theme of the gospel: not by works of the law, but only
by faith is man justified.

The neglect of Paul in the middle ages was not the result
of a direct denial of his significance.   Paul's letters did not
go untouched.   Thomas Aquinas has left us a commentary
on Romans.   But one need only lay this commentary alongside of that of Luther to become aware of a profound difference
between them.   The words of Paul were exegeted by Roman
Catholic scholars, but they were not allowed to function in
their original, radically evangelical power.   It was first in
the Reformation   that the old words of Paul came through
again in unprecedented religious clarity.   They unleashed a
storm over Europe, and yet brought peace and comfort to a
generation of restless souls.   Thomas wrote of Romans 5:1:
"It is not that faith precedes grace, but far more that faith
originates in grace, since faith is the first operation of grace
in us."[3]   It would be too much to expect a revolution in the

---

3. *Des Heiligen Thomas von Aquin Kommentar zum Römerbrief* (published by Helmut Fahsel), 1927, p. 157.

thought and confession of the Church to be ignited by such words as these. Thomas says about Abraham whose faith was reckoned to him for righteousness "that the righteousness which God accounts to a man is not that ascribed to external works, but to the inward faith of the heart which God alone sees."[4] This type of interpretation and its antithesis between the "external" and "inward" aspects of justification does not begin to approach the depth of Reformation exegesis.

We must understand that it was the Word of God which broke the fetters of tradition binding Roman Catholic exegesis. We must understand this if we are to avoid the theological opium of traditionalism and confessionalism. The Reformation confession of *sola fide* points us irresistibly to the Holy Scriptures themselves. And, in turn, it is only the Scriptures which may be allowed to decide whether the Reformation *sola fide* was the fruit of a fragmentary perspective or a real revival of the whole gospel.

* * *

Needless to say, Paul himself was profoundly convinced that the gospel he preached was no innovation, no new theological twist of his own. In writing to the Galatians he made this most emphatic: "But though we, or an angel from heaven should preach unto you any gospel other than that which we preached unto you, let him be anathema" (Gal. 1:8). He, too, is bound hand and foot to the received gospel. The gospel is untouchable, having arisen neither from his nor any other man's personal experiences. Whatever apostolic authority he has is dependent upon and relative to the fact that he received the revelation from Jesus Christ (Gal. 1:12). He feels himself consumed by the doctrine of Christ, so much so that, in a way foreign to any subjective arbitrariness, he is compelled under threat of condemnation to preach it (I Cor. 9:16).

---

4. *Ibid.*, p. 134.

His preaching, then, is not a segment of the gospel, magnified and become grotesque in its blown-up disproportion. He preached the whole of the gospel. This is, of course, not to be taken quantitatively, as though all sermons preached since Paul should be a repetition of what he has said, or as though the other apostolic witnesses to Christ were superfluous. He preached the evangel in its totality, but other inspired books are neither unnecessary nor extraneous. "And there are also many other things which Jesus did, the which if they should be written every one, I suppose that even the world itself would not contain the books that should be written" (John 21:25). Quantitatively, John says, his gospel is not adequate. There is a certain quantitative restraint in apostolic writing and speaking, a selectiveness, which is most apparent, perhaps, in the four gospels. They draw from the inexhaustible resources of the life and death and resurrection of Jesus Christ, but the revelation must be defined by a certain form (Eph. 3:10). Furthermore, even in *apostolic* speech, knowledge is only in part; there is a limitation marked off by God Himself. Paul did not say everything and could not have said everything, nor did his letters grow to a great series of tomes. There is room for others in the New Testament, for a rich pluriformity in approach to and explanation of the one complete salvation.[5] In each letter — and this is the beauty of the New Testament — another light is played on that salvation. Not a brush stroke is added to the portrait; we are but given another perspective of the finished work.

This is why Paul can claim to preach the full gospel and why he places that gospel in opposition to every other. When he left the elders of Ephesus he was able to say not only that he "shrank not from declaring unto you anything that was profitable," but also that he "shrank not from declaring unto

---

5. Cf. what Christ said to Martha about one thing being necessary in the midst of many things (Luke 11:41, 42).

you the whole counsel of God" (Acts 20:20, 27).[6] Naturally Paul has no pretensions to having exhaustively known and preached the whole mind of God in any crudely quantitative sense. He means that he has preached the clear and authoritative existential message by which the hearer is placed relentlessly in the situation of complete responsibility and in which he at the moment of hearing stands naked before God. Not an atomistic conglomeration of a number of truths, but a message of salvation — this is what Paul preaches, with the directness of an irrefutable witness. When Paul says that he left nothing unsaid which was useful he adds that he testified "both to Jews and to Greeks repentance toward God, and faith toward our Lord Jesus Christ" (Acts 20:21). The latter clause qualifies the former. Paul was no less plenary in his preaching to the Corinthians when he insisted that he knew nothing among them save Jesus the Crucified (I Cor. 2:2). Thus, with the others, Paul preached the one gospel in manifold modes of expression and in various situations, but always with one theme — God's grace directed to man in his estrangement from God.

This is why it is so wrong to speak of a one-sided Pauline theology. It is also why there is no Pauline, as over against a Petrine or Johannine, Christianity. This is not to make a monotone of the biblical witness; it is to insist that the witnesses are all in the same key.

Paul's own universality and multiformity forbids anyone to brand him as one-sided. The tendency to react to one error by exaggerating its opposite to the point of exclusiveness, a tendency which has been fateful in the Church and her doctrine, is quite foreign to Paul. He might have been tempted by the Galatians to exaggerate justification by faith until

---

6. In connection with Paul's being constrained to preach, under weight of condemnation if he did not, note his remark in verse 26 of this chapter: "I am pure from the blood of all men." Calvin has no doubt but that he had in mind how God told Ezekiel (Ezek. 3:18 ff.) that Ezekiel would be guilty of their blood if he did not call the godless to repentance. Cf. Calvin's commentary on the Acts of the Apostles, *in loco.*

it became his only message, or by the Corinthians to exaggerate sanctification until it eclipsed the *sola fide*. In fact, however,
neither truth gives place to the other.   There is a golden chord
running through and binding Romans 6 and 12, I Corinthians
6, and Galatians 5.   Paganism, Judaism, Christian heretics,
and sinful believers — Paul encountered them all.   But he
was never driven by any of them to one-sidedness.   He got at
them all by way of the radical critique of the gospel and the
ever appropriate warning implied in it.

One-sidedness in the Church thrives on fragments.   The
fragments intoxicate their devotees until they lose sight of
the whole.   One-sided enthusiasm has often been a reaction
to a very real evil in the Church (Remember, Marcion was
against nomism and legalism!).   But it usually lacks a
balanced translation of the whole counsel of God and thus
often substitutes evil for evil.

Paul was not a victim of this tendency.   When he warned
the Thessalonians against neglecting their responsibilities in
their anticipation of the return of Christ, he did not lose his
vision for the future.   When he was concerned about people
irreligiously striving for the righteousness of the law, he did
not devaluate the law of God (Rom. 7:12).

His message did not make the other apostles superfluous,
nor did the others' him.   On the other hand, the apostles
do not each contribute a certain number of truths which, all
summed up, make up the whole matter.   The preaching of
the apostles has its place in the history of revelation, and is,
in turn, influenced by that history.   The salvation they preach
is always essentially the same, although its application depends
much on the situation in which the message is brought.   The
difference is in the *ways* in which the salvation is proclaimed.
We can hardly avoid recognizing how much more profoundly
and extensively Paul reveals the mystery of Christ than Jude
does, yet we admit that they both have the same revealed
authority.   Sometimes a single, limited event or circumstance

calls for only a brief illumination by the light of the gospel. Paul's own letter to Philemon is a remarkable instance of this. Philemon, revealing and instructive as it is, hardly reaches the high point in the history of revelation of the letters to the Romans and the Galatians. Revelation is related to the concrete, historical situation that occasions a given writing, and the situation is in turn mirrored in the piece. We see this in the difference between the preaching of Jesus and the preaching of Paul. It does not diminish the authority of Christ's preaching to admit that Paul plunged deeply into various questions which Jesus merely touched upon. The greater profundity of Paul's treatment is defined by history, by the growth of the Church after the coming of the Holy Spirit and by many new questions provoked by many new errors. Christ Himself suggested this growth: "I have yet many things to say unto you, but ye cannot bear them now. Howbeit when he, the Spirit of truth, is come, he shall guide you into all the truth: for he shall not speak from himself; but what things soever he shall hear, these shall he speak: and he shall declare unto you the things that are to come" (John 16:12, 13). Christ through His Spirit leads the apostles into the greater depth (John 16:14). In this entire development the one, unchangeable gospel is only made more explicit. But while this is true, the historical mutations and inflections within the development remain significant. The letters of the New Testament are not to be robbed of their own individuality.

In Paul all the threads of the history of revelation were drawn together. He met situations in Rome and Galatia which occasioned explicit illumination of the gospel contrast between law and grace. In this contrast the heart, the essential character of the gospel was at stake. Melanchthon's *Apology* said rightly that the doctrine of justification opened the door to the Holy Scriptures, for it meant by this that justification was the substructure of salvation. Naturally, even at this point, it is quite possible to force one's own ideas on the Scriptures. But, let a man fully recognize and confess the bedrock of salvation in Paul's message and he shall be safeguarded from one-sidedness.   For this fundament is not a fraction of the gospel.   It is an insight into the heart of God's salvation, given by the Holy Ghost.

When Paul's eyes were first opened to the gospel, he saw against the background of his own former life that the law was fatal.   This does not mean that Paul accepted an anti-thesis between law and grace.   Paul was concerned with actual situations.   Men were knocking themselves out trying to please God by their own righteousness.   In respect to this situation Paul opposed grace to law, or rather the righteous-ness of faith to the righteousness of the law.   This antithesis is identical with the gospel; with it the gospel stands or falls. From our vantage point, we may be grateful for the providence that brought Paul, the Pharisee who had sought his own righteousness with such restless zeal, to defend the gospel of grace in situations so specific as to force his letters to be concrete.

There is, then, a unique relation between Paul's past life and his radical presentation of the gospel.   Paul describes his past life thus: "as touching the law, a Pharisee; as touch-ing zeal, persecuting the church; as touching the righteousness which is in the law, found blameless" (Phil. 3:5, 6).   When he saw his past life, his zeal, his striving for righteousness, as a persecution, not of the Church only, but of Jesus Christ, he counted it all loss and shame.   The excellence of the knowl-edge of Christ had exposed the vanity of his former life. The "way of salvation" was something entirely different.   A new world was open to Paul in Christ.   He was found in Christ, "not having my own righteousness of the law, but the right-eousness through faith in Christ" (Phil. 3:9).   Striving for righteousness, Paul had persecuted Christ and the *way* of Christ (Acts 22:4).   But the judgment of mercy fell on his striving. He saw Christ; and Christ's appearance divided his life into two phases, a division which defined and governed his entire life and work. His conversion pointed to the trans-subjective, to the divine initiative of grace which renewed his life. After that, when Paul spoke of his own life, he directed all the attention to this divine mercy: "howbeit for this cause I obtained mercy, that in me as chief might Jesus Christ show forth all his longsuffering, for an ensample of them that should thereafter believe on him unto eternal life" (I Tim. 1:16). This Pharisee, this plague to the Church, had become now an example of sheerest mercy, a herald of the Kingdom of God's grace. With tenderest affection, he witnessed among his own people to the "hope of Israel" (Acts 28:20), to save them from their own blind zeal and to turn them from their futile search for righteousness. He points Israel to another righteousness, the hidden meaning of Israel's own history. As a "chosen instrument" (Acts 9:15), he also brings Christ's name before the heathen; he proclaims it before kings. He is even allowed to suffer for the sake of the Name (Acts 9:15, 16). He struggles with all who impoverish the gospel by forcing the converted pagans into a pattern of legalistic methodism (Gal. 3:1). He leads his readers into the depths of mysteries. Yet, he directs the distressed jailor to the utter simplicity of total salvation — belief in the Lord Jesus (Acts 16:31).

This is Paul, the preacher of the nonsense which is wiser than the wisdom of men and of the weakness which is stronger than the strength of men (I Cor. 1:25). He declares that God is not known by the wisdom of the world, that God has made this wisdom foolishness. In all the nuances and accents of his witness, this one theme remains, the one stumbling block for Jews and Greeks, the theme of righteousness by faith in Christ. "By faith alone" — this was a humiliation for the zealous disciples of the "righteousness of the law." "The cross of Christ" — this was an offence to the disciples of "human wisdom." Paul, too, in his "wisdom" and "zeal" had known the gospel as a stumbling block, but, converted from Satan to the living God (Acts 26:18), he could write: "but God chose the foolish things of the world, that he might put to shame them that are wise; and God chose the weak things of the world, that he might put to shame the things that are strong; and the base things of the world, and the things that are despised, did God choose, yea and the things that are not, that he might bring to nought the things that are: that no flesh should glory before God" (I Cor. 1:27-29).

* * *

It was this gospel that Paul preached, which, in its integrity, was brought to life again by the Reformation. It was not merely one neglected aspect that Luther and Calvin recaptured. They saw the *whole* in a new light. In studying the Reformation, one is struck by the remarkable correspondence between Paul's struggle against Judaism in both its gross and its refined work-righteousness and the Reformation struggle against human merit. The struggle of the sixteenth century is, of course, quite dependent upon that of the first. It was the gospel that reached its climax in Paul's preaching which roused itself in the Reformation and shook off the shackles of the contrition and attrition technique, the system of penance, and the idea of merit which had kept it bound during much of the middle ages. Paul did not fight historical Judaism because it stubbornly clung to an expendable tradition and practiced customs unessential to true religion. Paul recognized the legal conditions for entry into Christendom for what they were, an obtrusion into Christianity which changed its essential character. He resolved the dilemma of "law" and gospel with the doctrine of unalloyed grace. This was at bottom the same dilemma which Rome set before the Reformation and which the reformers wrestled with so fruitfully.

There was indeed an ever present danger of one-sidedness in the Reformation. Luther did not always escape it. He has, for instance, been accused of reading the ideas of Paul into the writings of John. He came to John, it is said, by way of Paul. This could mean that he simply refused to disjoin John from the central theme of the gospel. But Luther undoubtedly did more than that. He tended to see in John's work the very same pitched battle against work-righteousness as that which Paul waged. John was not always allowed to speak for himself. This was one-sided. But that does not mean that the Reformation doctrine of *sola fide-sola gratia* itself is one-sided. For the doctrine is not exclusive with Paul. It is only that Paul was faced with concrete situations in which he had to demonstrate peculiar apostolic intolerance of other gospels which sought to replace the gospel of grace. There are significant differences amongst the various Bible writers, differences defined by the various situations into which the gospel was sent; for this reason it is surely impermissible to interpret John by way of Paul or vice versa. But the differences lie only in the *manner* of explicating the one fundament of salvation. When Luther read Paul into John's writings, he was not — in spite of errors in exegetical detail — distorting the fundamental message of salvation through God's grace, for this was common to John and Paul. It has never been shown that Luther fundamentally misunderstood John. Nor can he have done so, since the heart of the matter for John as well as for Paul was the priority of divine grace and love.

This one gospel of grace, appearing in the New Testament in as many variations as there are writers and situations, was common to all the inspired authors. It was this gospel, this central theme of gracious salvation, that the reformers reclaimed and proclaimed.

The relation between Peter and Paul requires an explanation also, since, as we have observed, it is sometimes supposed that Peter poses as a sort of mediator between Judaistic and non-Jewish Christianity, or between justification through works and justification through faith. This is, however, a complete misunderstanding of Peter. That there was some tension between Peter and Paul is clear enough from what Paul wrote in Galatians 2 about his withstanding Peter to the face. It seemed that while Peter had found it permissible to sit at the table with former pagans, some of James's disciples refused to join him out of fear for the "circumcised." This made Peter timid, too, and he compromised with the scrupulous Jews. This was not a matter of fundamental difference between Peter and Paul. It was simply a case in which Peter temporarily lost the courage of his convictions and scrupled where the gospel demanded a holy unscrupulousness. Peter, become a flincher in fear, had broken the intimate fellowship with non-Jewish Christians that he had enjoyed. Paul accused him, quite rightly, then, of hypocrisy. Peter's actions gave the impression to others less mature that the Gentiles were second class Christians, not to be approved by the Jews until they had assumed certain of the Jewish laws and prescriptions. Paul was deathly afraid of the influence that Peter's actions would have on others and had already had in the case of Barnabas.

All this, however, does not constitute a permanent opposition between the Petrine and the Pauline gospel. We read nothing in Galatians 2 as to the upshot of Paul's complaint,[7] and nowhere in the New Testament do we find anything that smacks of a permanent difference in the apostolic preaching of Paul and Peter.

Luther occupied himself for a time with the conflict between Peter and Paul. He saw it as being relevant to the place of

---

7. Cf. Meyer, *Kommentar zum Galatiersbrief,* 1886, p. 157: "We have every reason to believe that the consequence of [Paul's] speech was favorable. Naturally, this could not prevent those Judaists who were inimicably disposed toward Paul from using their recollection of this incident at Antioch as an appeal in later years to the judaizing Peter as against Paul, the Gentile's apostle."

the law in Christianity and to the position of Peter in the Church. He rejected Jerome's idea that the affair involved only an apparent conflict and says, with Augustine, that such a construction does violence to the very lucid text. Peter's action, according to Luther, posed a threat to Christian liberty. Paul is supposed to have opposed Peter "on behalf of one of the most important articles of Christian teaching, which Peter almost undid with his hypocrisy."[8] Having said this, Luther then turns to the Pope, who, he says, is worse than Peter, for he "turned the gospel into idle legalism." Luther used the example of Peter's error at Antioch to fight the notion of papal infallibility. But this hardly means that Luther, in reaction, turned the gospel into a one-sided Pauline theology, no more than Paul's censure of Peter caused him, in reaction, to swing back to another extreme.

Peter later referred to Paul as "our beloved brother." He recognized the profundity of Paul's letters and said that those ignorant and unsteadfast people who misconstrue them do so to their own destruction (II Pet. 3:16). When we listen to Peter preach, we hear the pure tones of sovereign grace. He is anything but a mediating figure between those who preach justification by works and those who preach justification by faith. Redemption through "the precious blood, as of a lamb without blemish and spot, even the blood of Christ" (I Pet. 1:19); appropriation of Christ through faith (I Pet. 2:7); the One Name through whom we may be saved (Acts 4:12) — these are what Peter preached. The affair in Antioch was a sorry episode in Peter's experience, but little more than that. "And when there had been much questioning, Peter rose up, and said unto them, Brethren, ye know that a good while ago God made choice among you, that by my mouth the Gentiles should hear the word of the gospel and believe. And God, who knoweth the heart, bare them witness, giving them the Holy Spirit, even as he did unto us" (Acts 15:7-9). That

---

8. Luther, *Kommentar zum Galatiersbrief* (edition of 1856), p. 162.

is the witness of Peter, and, in complete agreement with Paul, he adds: "But we believe that we shall be saved through the grace of the Lord Jesus, in like manner as they" (Acts 15:11). Peter and Paul are fellows in a common task of proclaiming the gospel which all biblical witness has in common.

This fellowship is the one foundation on which all the apostles desire to build. All their letters focus on the one act of redemption in Christ, suggesting again the unity within the variety of the New Testament witness. The individuality of the writers is not allowed to run into individualism. Individualism stems from and fosters competitive goals and designs. The New Testament writers, however, are unified, without loss of their individuality, by the One sent from the Father for the redemption of the world. They find their harmony in this divine design, and in it, together present an antithesis to the vain righteousness which is according to the works of the law. The Reformation continually appealed to Paul only because in him the contrast between work-righteousness and faith-righteousness comes to the sharpest religious clarity. That appeal certainly did not imply that the reformers neglected the resources of the four evangelists, nor that they were deaf to the other apostolic witnesses. Luther, for instance, felt at home in the letters of Peter, who translated the gospel of grace in his own way while led by the same Holy Spirit as was Paul. Thus, the theology of the Reformation was not the theology of Paul, anymore than the theology of Peter. It was the theology, in brief, of the unmerited grace of God, which is to say, the theology of the whole New Testament. The theology of Paul was no more than this. Let it be said that the Reformation was most deeply influenced by the letters of Paul. It need mean only that the Reformation, like Paul, did not fall victim to a fatal, subjective one-sidedness.

* * *

We should pause a moment for a consideration of the sharp antithesis that Paul makes between justification by the works

of the law and justification by faith.   This antithesis is the
heavy accent sounded in Romans and Galatians which the
Reformation heard and translated in terms *sola fide-sola gratia.*
"We reckon therefore that a man is justified by faith apart
from the works of the law" (Rom. 3:28).   "Being therefore
justified by faith, we have peace with God through our Lord
Jesus Christ" (Rom. 5:1).   ". . . because by the works of the
law shall no flesh be justified in his sight" (Rom. 2:20).   "Yet
knowing that a man is not justified by the works of the law
but through faith in Jesus Christ, even we believed on Christ
Jesus, that we might be justified by faith in Christ, and not
by the works of the law: because by the works of the law
shall no flesh be justified" (Gal. 2:16).   "If righteousness
is through the law, then Christ died for nought" (Gal. 2:21).
"Now that no man is justified by the law before God, is evident: for, The righteous shall live by faith" (Gal. 3:11).

In the profound antithesis that he indicates in these texts,
Paul is concerned to direct his reader to the salvation which
is in Christ.   His opposition to every method of obtaining
salvation by means of a legal formula is obstinately intense
because he sees such techniques as competitors to Christ.   His
rebuff to work-righteousness — the illegitimate son of legalism — is not directed against the law, but against the sinful
man who thinks himself good enough to obtain righteousnes:
before God and who uses the law as a ladder.   Israel did this
when she began to look on the law as the way of salvation
par excellence.   Paul sees the utter impossibility of this and
posits the way of faith as the true alternative.

If it were possible to obtain the righteousness of God
through obedience to the law, says Paul, Christ's death would
have been *for nothing* (Gal. 2:21).[9]   A new way, the way of

---

9. Cf. G. Dehn, *Gesetz oder Evangelium,* 1934, p. 92: "worthless, base-
less, senseless."   Paul uses the word *doorean,* the same word found in
John 15:25: "They hated me *without a cause."*   Cf. Meyer, *Kommentar
zum Galatiersbrief,* p. 156: "It would have been an act of extravagance,
if that which it was intended to accomplish could be obtained by the way
of the law."

faith in Christ, to become righteous before God would be quite
superfluous if man were able to earn it through the law (Rom.
3:28). God would be guilty of throwing Himself away. The
absolute antithesis that Paul insists on between the two ways
of becoming righteous in God's eyes coincides with the two
epochs of his own life: before and after he met Jesus Christ.
Before his conversion he worked for his own righteousness;
afterward, he accepted that of Christ. Everything which was
formerly essential became worthless thereafter.[10] The old
way came to a dead end; the new began at his encounter with
Christ. The nature and the direction of the new way of salvation was defined in *Him*. There could be nothing more
radical than this antithesis. It is not construed as the fruit
of Paul's own experience; it is a root essential of the gospel.
The other apostles may have given it other dress, but they
are one with Paul as to the indispensibleness of this *way*, the
way made manifest in Christ.

The sweet comfort and alarming force of Paul's antithesis
has perennial significance; the question "how can I be saved,"
is every man's and hits the heart of every man's life. It defines
his life for him.

The antithesis works in force always, but in a manner appropriate to the particular garb which the righteousness of
works may happen to wear. As it made its point with the
overt demands of Judaism, it scores as well any pious construction of work-righteousness, even if it be set up against
the background of grace. The way of work-righteousness,
according to Paul, leads to nowhere. Judging from the
profound and perpetual earnestness with which he views it,
Judaism was, for Paul, more a symptom of the threat to grace
inherent in man's sinful self-importance than a passing attitude
of his own day. There is none righteous, no, not one. There
is none that understandeth. There is none that seeketh after
God (Rom. 3:10, 11). Jew and Greek alike is sinful, and

10. Cf. K. Barth, *Erklärung des Philipperbriefes*, 1928, p. 97.

there is no fear of God in him (Rom. 3:18). Paul's attack is not directed first of all against the proud, unbroken humanity of the world, whose autonomy and self-sufficiency abides undisturbed outside of Christ. He strikes hardest at the peculiar self-righteousness of the religious man.

He champions instead the true, wholly other righteousness, that righteousness which counts with God — the righteousness of faith. A critical nuance is discernible in Paul's strategy at this point: no righteousness through *works*, but true righteousness through *faith*. Is this a sleight of hand which slips in one human medium in place of another, human faith for human works? Both seem to carry the taint of stipulations without which righteousness is not to be obtained. It almost suggests that Paul disqualifies human works only to substitute another requirement, the act of faith.

To interpret Paul in this way would be to fall prey to a distortion that has often been death to biblical spirituality. Through this perversion of Paul's intent Christians have been cheated of the comfort of God's justification and have fallen into a proud self-consciousness that comes to rest, really, in self-righteousness. Naturally, for in this garbling of Paul's words, works and faith are put on the same shelf, while the righteousness wholly of grace becomes a mis-placed and forgotten article. When he is so construed, Paul must need say: "then Christ died for naught." Paul did not dedicate his life to espouse faith as a human work in place of another, less promising, work — that of the law. He poured out his heart in preaching that Christ did not die for nought. His message was an appeal for a radical conversion, a turn-about from *all* human works of self-righteousness to the cross of Christ. This profound revolution was his perpetual theme.

*   *   *

The Scriptures do not give a uniform, monotoned expression to the righteousness which is by faith. For instance, Paul says that Abraham received the sign of circumcision as a seal of the righteousness *of* faith (Rom. 4:11, *tees pisteos*). He speaks as well of the righteousness *out of* (or *by*) faith (*ek pisteos,* Rom. 9:30; 10:6; Gal. 5:5) and of *through* faith (*dia pisteos,* Phil. 3:9). We sometimes find two of these expressions in a single verse (cf. Rom. 3:30; Gal. 2:16; 3:18), as though we are justified both out of (or by) *and* through faith.

Within these variations, one central theme is common — the intimate correlation between faith and justification. Nowhere does faith take on the guise of a work, of human achievement which in one way or another effectuates justification. The prepositions *through* (*dia*) and *of* or *by* (*ek*) point us to the way in which man is granted salvation in Christ. In Galatians 2:16 *through faith* and *of faith* are parallel. The shading in terminology offers no real difficulty, since no preposition is ever used with such a grammatical case of the noun *faith* as to render necessary a translation like *because of* or *by reason of* faith. Faith is never put forward as a work of creativity, of mediacy, of merit. It is never given as a ground of justification.[11]

The expressions *of* and *through faith* direct us to the objectivity of God's grace in Christ, which, of and through faith, is recognized and received as wholly divine grace.

In Romans 3:22 we find the expression "through faith of Jesus Christ.[12] Greijdanus writes that Paul uses this phrase to say that Christ is not only the object of faith, but that He defines that faith as to content, essence, and activity. Be this

---

11. Cf. S. Greijdanus on Gal. 2:12 (*Commentaar op Galatiërs,* p. 174): "From this interchange of preposition and case it appears that *pistis* is given not as *ground,* but as *instrument* of justification. Neither Paul nor any other N. T. writer says, *dia pistin, because of* faith." Cf. also Zahn, *Römerbrief,* p. 240, note 86.

12. Tr. note: This paragraph assumes the reading as given above, which is also that of the King James Version. The American Standard Version, otherwise used in this book, gives the reading "through faith *in* Jesus Christ." The difference turns on a point in textual evaluation.

so, it underscores the nature of the way of faith. This is substantiated by the rest of Paul's sentence: this righteousness of God through faith of Jesus Christ is "unto all them that believe."

We could speak here of the instrumental function of faith, or of the *way* of faith on which the signs point to Christ alone. It is as when Christ Himself spoke to Paul in their encounter: "that they may turn from darkness to light, and from the power of Satan unto God, that they may receive remission of sins and an inheritance among those that are sanctified *by faith in me*" (Acts 26:18; cf. Acts 24:14). It is this idea of "the way on which" that we must hold before us in considering the relation between faith and justification. For the moment we need only say that attention is focused not on faith in itself as a human act, but on Christ and His grace which is seen only in faith.

A consideration of Abraham, the father of the faithful, may help us to understand the nature of the righteousness which is of faith. Our thought turns as a matter of course to Paul's citation from Genesis 15: "And Abraham believed God and it was reckoned unto him for righteousness" (Gen. 15:6; Rom. 4:3; 4:9; 4:22; Gal. 3:6; James 2:23). This phrase has occasioned spirited debates in the past. The question it poses is: How is the relation between faith and justification made manifest in the figure of Abraham?

Adolf Deissmann once felt it necessary to ward off a misunderstanding of Paul such as would construe justification as "God's reward for the human performance of faith."[13] He suggests, however, that Paul himself gave occasion for such abuse. His use of the term *reckoned*, borrowed, says Deissmann, from the Septuagint, suggests a mechanical exchange and implies an achievement of faith automatically rewarded with justification. The word itself is un-Pauline, and Paul

---

13. A. Deissmann, *Paulus, Eine kultur- und religionsgeschichtliche Studie,* 1925, 2nd ed., p. 132.

is hemmed in by the use of somebody else's term. It must be read, therefore, only as informed by the main body of Paul's own theology. Read the whole of Paul, and it is as plain as day that faith is no achievement presented to God, but a divine work performed on the man in Christ. "Faith is not a preliminary stipulation for justification; it is man's experience of it."

But if, as Deissmann maintains, the idea is foreign to Paul, why did the apostle fence himself in with it? Michaelis relevantly asks, "How could Paul willingly lay himself open to such misunderstanding?"[14]

The question, then, is whether the idea of an *achievement* of faith has been smuggled into Paul's writing through this term. The answer is definitely negative. Nothing in the books of Romans or Galatians carries a hint of such an idea. This is apparent in Romans 4:3 ff. Here Paul, after recalling the example of Abraham, directly sets up an antithesis between works, with reward according to debt, and the reckoning of faith as righteousness unto those who do not work but do believe in Him who justifies the ungodly. Paul could not have shown us more clearly that the righteousness reckoned to Abraham is in complete harmony with divine justification based on grace alone.

Certainly there is good reason to give Paul a careful ear before interrupting his argument with a quick polemic. That Paul had no difficulty with the term *reckoned*, taken from Genesis 15:6, appears from the fact that he cites David in the same breath with his reference to Abraham: "Blessed are they whose iniquities are forgiven, And whose sins are covered. Blessed is the man to whom the Lord will not reckon sin" (Rom. 4:7, 8). It is striking that the subjective side of the correlation is not mentioned. Here we have only the divine judgment over man in merciful pardon. This, natur-

---

14. W. Michaelis, "Rechtfertigung aus dem Glauben bei Paulus" in *Festgabe für A. Deissmann zum 60. Geburtstag*, 1927, p. 124.

ally, does not mean that faith is without significance; but it does indicate that faith cannot presume to count as a human achievement. Again, in Galatians 3:6, right after Paul sets the works of the law in opposition to the gospel of faith, he brings up Abraham's faith as having been reckoned to him for righteousness. Obviously, his intent is not to diminish the opposition, but to establish it.

The nature of faith, just because it is directed to God, rules out all work-righteousness, including faith when it is conceived as a parallel or substitute for the works of the law. Paul discusses the reckoning of Abraham's faith unto righteousness in the same context as the justification of the ungodly. This suggests that Abraham's justification, too, was a gracious declaration of pardon rather than a reward for achievement. Abraham's status was that of uncircumcision. Circumcision came only later, as a seal of the righteousness which was reckoned to him as uncircumcised. Through faith alone! It is thus that Abraham became the father of all believers.

Certainly Abraham is not the prototype of legal perfection.

Judaism, fossilized in its legalism, might have so considered him. But Genesis and Paul never. A prototype of meritorious exploitation of the law would have been strangely set in the great chapter on the justification of the ungodly. He would then have been the worker rewarded according to debt. But Abraham is at home in Romans 4 just because his righteousness was only that of faith, and thus exclusively the boon of divine promise. Lifted out of the cell of self by God's promise, abandoning himself to God's keeping, overpowered by the divine Word — that is how Paul sees Abraham. That is the believing man. He heard the call of the Lord to leave his land, and he left (Gen. 12:1 ff). He heard the word of promise in the years of his age, and he believed the unbelievable (Gen. 15:5). He grasped the promise — as he was gripped by it — and he was sure that what God promised He

had the power to perform. This is why it was reckoned to
him for righteousness (Rom. 4:22). This faith — Abraham
giving God the glory (Rom. 4:20) — and justification are
bound together. The word *reckon* is used "for our sakes also
unto whom it shall be reckoned, who believe on him that
raised Jesus our Lord from the dead, who was delivered up
for our trespasses, and was raised for our justification" (Rom.
4:24, 25). The way of salvation is unveiled before our eyes.
The Scripture holds Abraham up before us that we may see
the mystery of our own justification.

If, then, God does not reckon faith as having achieved
righteousness, what does Paul mean?

The "traditional" Reformed exegesis of the passage in
question has come under heavy fire. It is described as saying
that God counts as righteous what in reality is unrighteous.
The impression is that God acts *as though* the sinner were
righteous, while actually the sinner is just that, a sinner. Thus,
God's judgment is a fictitious one. The Reformed exegete
presumably comes to this portion of Scripture from his hand-
book of dogmatics, and fits Paul to the measure of the
theological model. While Scripture really says that Abraham
is justified through his faith, Reformed dogmatic-exegesis
says he is not. This critique has an appearance of weight,
especially where it is contended that Scripture plainly says that
faith itself is accounted to Abraham for righteousness. This
does not mean that every critic of the Reformed interpretation
of this passage seeks to invest faith with a meritorious efficacy.
Nevertheless Reformed exegesis at this point *is* charged with
having closed its eyes to the great significance of active faith.
The objective basis in Christ's righteousness for our justification is so heavily underscored, it is charged, that faith gets
hardly any recognition. Faith, we are told, should be seen
as the subjective righteousness which is produced by the
objective righteousness of Christ and as that which demon-

strates our participation in Christ to be not fictitious but real.[15]

Exegesis, naturally, ought not to be measured by dogmatics; but on purely exegetical grounds we are constrained to prefer the traditional exegesis of this passage. It alone, we judge, does justice to the text and to Paul's entire witness concerning the righteousness of faith. The basic error of the "new" exegesis is most evident in the distinction it would make between the objective righteousness of Christ and the subjective righteousness of the believer. This distinction is proscribed by the fact that, where Abraham is concerned, there is not a causal relationship between Christ's righteousness and the righteousness of faith, but a *correlative association* in which the subjectivity of faith has meaning and significance only as it lives off grace. This does not disguise a devaluation of faith. It only attempts to define its character. Only thus, in fact, does the instrumental character of faith come into its own. Bavinck has been criticised for writing: "The words 'faith was reckoned for righteousness' form an abbreviated expression for the truth that God reckons His own righteousness (poured out in Christ) to someone *in faith,* and on that basis pardons him."[16] For this Bavinck was accused of sleight of hand. His meaning is perfectly clear, however, if we keep in mind the Pauline correlation between faith and justification. In that correlation faith and its content are simply inseparable. We are prohibited from abstracting a "subjective righteousness of faith" from the imputed righteousness of Christ, since it is precisely His righteousness with which faith is concerned. Imputation of the righteousness of Christ does not mean that God takes due note of and makes proper response to a subjective righteousness possessed by Abraham and all believers. It is the act of His grace in

---

15. For such criticism see H. J. Jager, *Rechtvaardiging en zekerheid des geloofs,* 1939, and J. G. Woelderink, *De rechtvaardiging uit het geloof,* 1941.
16. H. Bavinck, *Gereformeerde Dogmatiek,* IV, p. 195.

Christ. "Righteousness is conferred upon the believer."[17] Dogmatic prejudice did not dominate the traditional exegesis. This is the Scriptural message of the relation between faith and grace.[18]

This divine judgment and imputation of righteousness governs Paul's entire argument. "The judgment has its locus in the gracious will of God, therewith every human insight which would vaporize the judgment by the word *merit* is gainsaid. What faith is in itself does not interest me."[19] Justification is not God's affirmative conclusion to His analysis of man's subjective righteousness; nor can such an analytical justification have a place alongside of justification in Christ. To give it such a place renders innocuous our perpetual protest against the emasculation of faith committed by nominalism.

The correlation between faith and justification is too profound to allow us to speak of faith as a distinctive righteousness besides the perfect righteousness in Christ. This suggests the existence of two distinctive righteousnesses and, perhaps contrary to the original intention, leaves us unable to distinguish between faith and a new law.

The mere fact that Paul speaks of "reckoning" is remarkable. Contrary to Deissmann, Paul here shed the clearest possible light on the gracious act of justification: faith justifies apart from all works of the law. Faith is not an independent function with even the slightest power to justify; but it is precisely *this* human position of impotency in contra-distinction to which the "reckoning according to grace" (and not according to debt or merit) is possible.[20]

This is why the traditional understanding of Paul ever continues to bolster the spirit. It is not conditioned by fear

---

17. Kittel, *Theologisches Wörterbuch zum N. T.*, IV, p. 292.
18. Cf. *ibid.*, p. 294.
19. *Ibid.*
20. Cf. *ibid.*, where this relationship is admirably put: "Because faith which throws itself in trust under the judgment and grace of the Cross is the only proper human position, God's judgment according to grace is given in correspondence."

of Arminianism, but it does provide the best possible counter-balance to this particular over-estimation of faith as a spiritual achievement. It is necessary to understand this if we are to understand Paul in his preaching of this correlation, of the human grasping which is really a being grasped, of this faith, which, in faith, knows only grace and not itself.

We do not mean to say that the correlation between faith and justification has now become rationally transparent. On the contrary. But we do touch here upon the mystery of the *sola fide* as God's arrangement through which we can under-stand — through faith — that we are not justified through human achievement, but through faith, and that it is *this* faith that knows not itself which God reckons to us for righteousness.

Imputation of righteousness now becomes clear. Here we do not see faith as a human achievement in the sense in which Judaism understood Genesis 15:6.[21] For the imputation of righteousness occurs quite apart from all works of the law. While Judaism kept a tally sheet of the works of the law, with an eye to rewards if the accounts balanced, Paul's thought excludes the possibility of such bookkeeping. If faith were to keep a record of itself, it would sacrifice its very nature as faith. For faith is disinterested in itself, and looks only to grace. It is this faith that is reckoned as righteousness. When Paul made use of the words from Genesis 15:6, he did so to express the wealth contained in *sola fide,* "through faith alone."

The criticism that Pauline justification is a fiction is once and for all unfounded. We have already noted that the con-fessions did not hesitate to use the phrase *as if* or *as though,* if by it they could give utterance to the completeness of the rule of divine grace over our lives. The phrase was intended to underscore the most comforting reality of life in Christ. There is nothing fictional about this; the correlation between

---

21. Cf. *ibid.*: "One does not go far wrong if he understands 'reckoned according to debt' as a description of the Judaistic Book of Merit."

faith and grace excludes anything unreal. As Heidland says, "Justification is not a fictional something, something less than reality."[22] God does not allow Himself to be either the perpetrator or the object of illusions. His "reckoning" is worlds removed from make-believe. But it is just as far removed from any meritorious prestige in human faith. It points us to the exclusive sovereignty of grace, that "gracious gift which comes to one who renounces every pretension of merit and throws himself on God, who justifies just that pretentionless sinner."[23] *Sola fide* and *hence sola gratia!*

Though Paul shared the gospel of sovereign grace with all the apostles, he did frame it in his own contextual and terminological mold. We have noted how he reached back into the Old Testament for such examples as Abraham and David. In Moses, too, he discovers the fundamental antithesis in which the only way of salvation is set apart. "For Moses writeth that the man that doeth the righteousness which is of the law shall live thereby. But the righteousness which is of faith saith thus . . ." (Rom. 10:5, 6). The lamp of instruction is ignited. The way of salvation is marked off. The word is with us, in our mouth and in our heart, "the word of faith which we preach" (Rom. 10:8, cf. Acts 13:38, 39). The way of salvation is the way of faith because it is the way of grace in Christ. Our faith and piety are not share-holders in grace; indeed, our faith, by its very nature, excludes itself from the administration of salvation. This way of salvation can be sketched from many perspectives, but no matter what the viewpoint, the subject is always the intimate correlation between grace and faith.

In apostolic simplicity, all this means is to call upon the name of Christ (Acts 9:14, 21); this is to be saved (Acts 2:21). Not to call upon this Name is to walk the way of self-justification; and this is the fiction, the "as if" of unbelief

---

22. In Kittel, *ibid.*
23. *Ibid.*

(Luke 18:9, cf. Luke 20:20). When Paul discovered the way of faith, the way closed to the wise and learned but opened to the child-like, he rediscovered the Old Testament as the message of God's grace apart from the works of the law. It is not as though the *term* justification were the important thing, for this divine reality is incarnated in language as rich as revelation. "Distil, ye heavens, from above, and let the skies pour down righteousness: let the earth open, that it may bring forth salvation, and let it cause righteousness to spring up together; I Jehovah, have created it" (Is. 45: 8, 9). He has prepared salvation for His own name's sake. Nothing takes precedence to this salvation (Deut. 7:7), for in it God's righteousness is revealed (Is. 56:1). The true Israel casts itself on this righteousness, knowing that in it alone is she redeemed (Ps. 31:1, Is. 1:17). Many sorrows fall to the wicked, but he that trusteth in the Lord shall be compassed by His lovingkindness (Ps. 32:10), and none of them that take refuge in Him shall be condemned (Ps. 34:22). Thus, the same reality of divine mercy is revealed whether the *term* justification is used or not. This is why Paul is at ease in the Old Testament, while knowing that in Christ the saving grace of God has now appeared (Titus 2:11).

Whenever Paul speaks of the justification which has come to us, there is a single refrain — Christ has not died in vain. All striving and grasping makes sense only when it has been taken hold of by Christ (Phil. 3:12). Our contribution amounts to precisely zero. Faith knows this and is thus true faith, given by God. For it knows that Christ died for us while we were yet sinners (Rom. 5:8, 10).

Justification on the ground of nothing is not a one-sided juridical concept. It is the preaching of grace, sheer, unalloyed, unmerited grace.

The so-called forensic, juridical, or declarative character of justification has occasioned a long debate running through the history of the Church. Its opponents have been legion. It is well to remember that many objections to declarative justification are part and parcel with a rejection of the substitutionary suffering and death of Jesus Christ. Terms common to jurisprudence have been used in connection with Christ's death: satisfaction, sufficiency, payment, purchase, ransom, and punishment. And these terms have made men angry.

But in much of the offense that has been taken, the deep religious motives behind the use of such terms were missed. They are not the sour fruits of a speculative dogmatics. They are the life blood of Scripture, and are voiced in the jubilation of the Church triumphant: Thou "didst purchase unto God with thy blood men of every tribe, and tongue, and nation" (Rev. 5:9). If we listen without pre-formed criticism to Paul's claim that Christ has not died in vain, that he has become a curse for us and for us has been made sin, we shall think twice before saying that it was a doctrine called forensic justification which precipitated the crisis of the Reformation. The Reformation insistence on justification has often been caricatured; according to the critics, it has made a cold system, an external scheme out of the salvation which is in Christ. It has even been charged that, with its objectivizing of justification, the Reformation still managed to intrude faith as a human condition of salvation.[24]

---

24. Cf. H. E. Weber, *Reformation, Orthodoxie und Rationalismus.* I, 1937, p. 96. Orthodoxy faces this charge from many sources. Cf. Kittel, *Theologische Wörterbuch zum N. T.,* I, p. 451 (*ara, katara*). Galatians 3:13 (where Paul speaks of Christ as becoming a curse for us) is the text discussed. Paul, it is said, "expostulates here an idea of vicarious punishment, but, to be sure, not in the orthodox sense, which sets the cross in the light of a purely objective juridical process between God and Christ and which does not touch anything human nor comprehend anything personal." In place of this impersonal concept, substitution is projected as the foundation of a new fellowship between God and ourselves, a relation which is "not only objective in the sense of a juridical possibility, but at the same time the actual re-establishment of this fellowship with us." Büchsel, the author of these remarks, conceives orthodoxy as teaching that substitution is an objective fact, to which human faith must thereupon be added, as when an inheritance lies ready and waiting, but for which actual acceptance is necessary for its possession. Faith then becomes a stipulated condition. However, orthodoxy

We need not enter into a discussion as to whether orthodox theology itself has given occasion for this reproach. We need only state forthrightly that declarative or forensic justification, as it was, on biblical grounds, understood by the Reformation, rules out the thought of faith as a meritorious condition of salvation. Forensic justification has to do with what is *extra nos*, with the imputation of what Christ has done on our behalf. This was, indeed, the original disposition of the Reformation.

The Reformed confession offers the strongest possible resistance against every entanglement of our salvation with a concept of faith watered down with a mixture of merit. Naturally, the confession cannot force the believer to honor grace in his faith. The human heart is deceitful in matters of grace and justification, as it is in everything. But the declarative character of justification does perpetually recall the pure correlation between faith and grace. He who ignores this recollection will tend to rationalize the correlation, and so doing will fasten proportionate attention to faith "in itself" as a subjective conditional function. The confession directs us away from such rationalizing, for it confesses grace apart from *any* work of the law, even a work clothed in the garment of faith.

* * *

Thus, in the forensic idea of justification the *sola fide-sola gratia* finds its purest incarnation. The doctrine of forensic justification embodies the gracious act of God in Christ Jesus, whom man can take to himself in faith alone. No special

has always fought against Arminianism and other forms of universalism in so far as they divide justification into a subjective and an objective sphere and so introduce faith as a condition. Orthodoxy has rejected this attempt to give to faith a meritorious character. For this reason, it is beside the mark to say of orthodoxy that it thinks "objectively" of substitution, as Büchsel does. We meet here, again, as so often we do, an argument that has not delved deeply enough into the religious motives of a theology which seeks to account for the correlation between the cross of Christ and faith.

preference for a juridical thought-scheme prevails over the doctrine. It is rather an unwearying recognition of God's righteousness and mercy. *Sola fide* is the orthodox justification doctrine; "that which gives it [i.e., faith] its significance in the act of justification is exclusively that which is alloted to it from beyond all subjectivity."[25] This is true of Reformed, as of Lutheran confessional development. The forensic concept of justification is not a "contraction of justification," and it is antithetical to the renewal of life no more than the thought of legal pardon is antithetical to the sweetness of the free life beyond prison doors. The grace of Christ, poured out on a lost world, is preached without creating a conflict between God's righteousness and His mercy. There is no tension here either, only divine harmony — the prophecy of Isaiah fulfilled: "Zion shall be saved through righteousness."

When Paul refers to the gospel as the "power of God unto salvation" he is evidently thinking of the righteousness of God which is revealed in the gospel. Romans 1:17, which makes this clear, is a text of unusual importance in the history of theology. For a long time Luther read this righteousness as the avenging and retributive righteousness of a severe and unmitigating judge. For years he lived uncomforted, his soul haunted by this specter, the idea that God's righteousness was a threat to the gospel of grace. As, however, Romans 1:17 became clear to him, he began to appreciate the concord of divine righteousness and mercy. It was the concord so manifest in Romans 3: "For all have sinned and fall short of the glory of God; being justified freely by his grace through the redemption that is in Christ Jesus: whom God sent forth to be a propitiation, through faith, in his blood, *to show his righteousness* because of the passing over of the sins done aforetime . . ." (Romans 3:23-25). So perfectly are divine righteousness and mercy married in the cross of Christ, that

---

25. W. Elert, *Morphologie des Luthertums*, I, p. 91.

Paul can say: "that he might himself be just, and the justifier of him that hath faith in Jesus" (Romans 3:26). The cross reveals the inner unity of God's judgment and grace.

The cross, then establishes God's righteousness, as it includes the divine judgment over Christ and the pardon of all who believe in Him. Here begins the new way of salvation, the way from which all achievement, all human accomplishment is barred. The way begins at the cross, God's act of holy love and commisseration in Jesus Christ. Righteousness triumphs in His holiness and mercy. Sin is not tolerated or winked at, the law is not abolished, and the righteousness of God not violated.

Reconciliation through Christ's cross broadcasts God's righteousness. For this reason, we can speak of justification only forensically. And for this reason, Paul's thought suggests the atmosphere of the *tribunal Dei*. It is not as though he wants to circumscribe the mystery of salvation in juridical categories. It is simply that in justification pardon appears in the context of accusation and guilt. "Who shall lay anything to the charge of God's elect? It is God that justifieth; who is he that condemneth?" (Romans 8:34, 35). "The employment of the forensic idea by Paul is consistent and incontrovertible."[26] Justification is the unmerited righteousness of the ungodly, the righteousness which the publican received and which set him apart from the Pharisee who justified himself and remained unjustified (Luke 18:14). For this reason, we are forced to dismiss such objections to forensic justification as are brought, for example, by Osiander, Karl Holl, and J. H. Newman. All the arguments against what is called the synthetic concept of justification have a common complaint — that the doctrine renders the veracity of God suspect. But this complaint is actually satisfied by the substitutionary passion of Christ. For God's judgment in the cross is fiction no more than was Christ's bitter suffer-

---

26. Kittel, *op. cit.* II, pp. 219 f.

ing and desolation. The fact that in the years succeeding the Reformation there has been an unremitting plea for an "analytical" concept of justification can be accounted for only as the leaven of an attenuated confession of the vicarious suffering of Christ. Whenever this confession comes into dispute, a problem is created as to how God really can justify the ungodly without amputation of His holiness and veracity. But where the confession of substitution is the living confession of the Church, forensic justification, rather than being a threat to God's truthfulness, is its splendid revelation.

*   *   *

The reformers consciously avoided a one-sided picture of the biblical message of salvation, and, rather than teach an exclusive "Pauline" theology, declared the simplicity and clarity of the way of salvation according to the whole Scriptures. But they maintained this simplicity against all opposition. One example of this tenacity was occasioned by the contest with Rome, especially when the Council of Trent rejected so emphatically the imputation of Christ's righteousness and therewith *sola fide*. This may be said without denying that Trent did attempt to give recognition to God's grace. In the opening passage of the sixth decree (on justification), Christ is confessed as Redeemer. God has given Him as Redeemer through faith in His blood (Council of Trent, VI, 2). Much stress is laid on the benefaction of His death and the merit of His suffering (Trent, VI, 3). Thereupon, justification is described as translation of man from the situation in which he is born, as child of Adam, into the status of grace, as child of God (Trent, VI, 4). This fundamental translation is then elucidated in its various relationships. Grace, standing at the beginning, precedes human merit and puts the sinner in a position to prepare his own justification through free acquiescence to and cooperation with this grace (Trent, VI, 5).

Faith is not discussed here. It is not brought up until the sixth chapter, where it is described as belief that that which is revealed is true (Trent, VI, 6). Faith is not all determining, not decisive, but only one phase of the way of salvation. From faith one proceeds to love. Justification is thus conceived as an inward, real process of renewal. It is "not only the forgiving of sins, but also sanctification and renewal of the inward man through the free acceptance of grace and of the gifts through which man becomes righteous in place of unrighteous, and a friend in place of an enemy" (Trent, VI, 7). Through infused righteousness the sinner is justified to the root of his being, really and effectively, so that he is not only counted as just, but in reality *is* just.[27] Justification occurs when the Holy Spirit is poured into the heart, and abides there.[28] Along with forgiveness, man receives by infusion faith, hope, and love. If hope and love were not added, faith could not unite him fully with Christ (Trent, VI, 7). Faith does have value, and we may say with Scripture that we are justified by faith, but then only in such a way that faith is the beginning of the way on which man arrives at salvation. Faith is the basis of salvation and the root of all justification. Without faith it is impossible to please God.[29] Faith is, thus, beginning, foundation, root . . .

We may be inclined to conclude from this that Trent closed the gap between Rome and the Reformation. But we are quite quickly disappointed. Immediately after this document on faith, Trent begins to inveigh against the idle confidence of the heretics (Trent, VI, 9) and to warn against the idle delusion that one is made an heir of Christ *sola fide*, through mere faith (Trent, VI, 11). Again, after the decrees, the canons reject the Reformed confession: "If any say that the sinner is justified through faith alone, in the sense that nothing

27. "et non modo reputamur sed vere justi nominamur et sumus" (VI, 7).
28. "atque ipsis inhaerat" (*ibid*).
29. "fides est humanae salutis initium, fundamentum et radix omnis justificationis sine qua impossibile est placere Deo" (VI, 7).

else is necessary that cooperates to obtain the grace of justification and that it is not necessary for the sinner to prepare himself by means of his own will, *anathema sit*" (Trent, VI, 9).

At the same time, the ban is placed on any who teach that man is justified through imputation of the righteousness of Christ, or through the forgiveness of sins exclusive of the grace and love which is infused in the heart through the Holy Ghost. Again, they are anathema who teach that justifying grace is nothing other than the good favor of God.[30] That justifying faith is only a trust in God's mercy, or in God who forgives sin for Christ's sake, or that justification is through such trust alone, is also rejected (Trent, VI, Canon 12).

The conflict over justification is focused as sharply here as is possible within Christian confessions. Trent threw at the Reformation not merely a rejection of antinomianism, but a confession in which infused grace and love are subsumed within justification. This is what Trent maintained in opposition to the Reformation, and it must be granted that they made the contrast lucid enough. For it was against this very depreciation of God's "favor" that the reformers bolted. They did not merely formulate justification as "only the favor of God." This might make it appear that something else might be posited alongside of this favor. Their position was not an opposition to love and good works, but the defense of the forensic and declarative character of justification, and of the righteousness of Christ *extra nos*. For this they drew sovereign grace around the problem of the human situation, and conceived man as encircled by grace. In this Lutheran and Calvinistic theologians were one. They saw and understood the debates that went on at the Council of Trent about twofold righteousness and clearly grasped why Rome was not prepared to make a concession. They perceived that Trent's respect for faith as the beginning, foundation, and root of

---

30. "esse tantum favorem Dei."

salvation could not hold back a radical condemnation of the Reformation, for they knew that when the chips were down, Rome would hold *infused* righteousness to be *the* justification.

The *Apology* has it quite otherwise. We receive pardon "through faith in Christ alone, not through love — though love follows where faith is present."[31] And Calvin writes, "I place [justification] outside of us, because we are righteous in Christ alone."[32] Can they, asked Calvin, show me one place where the commencement of our renewal is reckoned, in part or whole, by God as our justification? Calvin sets *sola fide* against Canon 2 of Trent, and in doing so does not argue from a one-sided solism which grants no worth to love and good works, but from a profound acknowledgment of the gracious disposition of God which enfolds all salvation.[33] They deny this favor of God, says Calvin, and make of justifying grace a human disposition,[34] though the words of Scripture are plain. For what else could Paul be speaking of in Romans 4 than this favor of God? In this way, the spearhead of the Reformation was aimed at every intrusion of the meritoriousness of works or of infused righteousness into grace.

The profound inner motivation of the conflict has not always been recognized by Rome.[35] She has set faith, hope, and love on the same plateau in the human situation and has failed to recognize the unique character of faith. In the same way, she set justification within a system of infused qualities. From this followed her rejection of what she called "merely a favorable disposition of God." Moral life and ethics were

31. J. T. Müller, *Bekenntnisschriften der evangelishe lutherische Kirche,* pp. 100, 108.

32. Calvin, *Acta Synoda Tridentum cum Antidoto,* Opera VII, p. 488.

33. *Ibid.,* p. 477: "Fides ergo sola est quae justificat; fides tamen quae justificat, non est sola."

34. *Ibid.,* p. 478.

35. Cf. for instance the confusion of Pighius who, in connection with the proposition that faith is "fiducia, qua in conscientia apprehendimus Christum coram Deo et in Christo patrem," exclaimed, "In conscience, before God, what can this be? Not one word of this is comprehensible." (In Weber, *op. cit.,* I, p. 132.)

considered in danger. Imputation was viewed as something
external and mechanical. And so the discussions between the
reformers and Rome at Regensburg in 1541 came to nothing.
Rome was zealous to rescue the ethical element from the
alien and extrinsic imputation doctrine, and to this end worked
out an ethico-dynamic medium of justification which actually
serves to emasculate the grace by which we are saved. The
reformers saw and rejected the very danger which later thinkers
cited as inherent in the orthodox Reformed doctrine of justification, the investiture of faith with the merit of works. They
set their sights on what was religiously at stake — the complete and sufficient grace of God for our salvation.

*   *   *

If the reformers wrestled with the Roman Catholic doctrine
of infused grace, they came as earnestly to grips with yet another form of analytical justification — the doctrine of
Osiander.

The Formula of Concord contains a spirited polemic against
this theologian, in which polemic we can discern a parallel
between Osiander's doctrine and that of Rome. For us, the
difference between Rome's infused righteousness and Osiander's "essential righteousness" is of comparatively slight
consequence. What is significant is that for Osiander, Christ,
according to His divine nature, dwells in our hearts, and there
constitutes our righteousness. With Osiander, as with Rome,
sanctification is the ground of justification. We are justified
through the reality of Christ in us. Calvin felt that Osiander
did not intend to replace the doctrine of unmerited justification
with his idea of essential righteousness, but that he nonetheless "involved it in such obscurity as darkens pious minds, and
deprives them of a serious sense of the grace of Christ."[36]
He points to Osiander's attempt to show that, according to
the Scriptures, Christ is one with us and we are one with

36. Calvin, *Institutes*, III, xi, 5.

Him, which, says Calvin, needs no proof. But Osiander became confused when he failed to observe the bond of this
unity. He was not satisfied with "that righteousness which
has been procured for us by the obedience and sacrificial death
of Christ, he imagines that we are substantially righteous in
God, by the infusion of his essence as well as his character."[37]

Calvin is apprehensive lest in this way we should be robbed
of justification, which alone is able to give us confidence of
our salvation. Justification and sanctification are indeed
inseparable, for Christ cannot be torn apart. But Osiander
confuses and mixes up this two-fold grace. He thereby em-
barasses Paul. While Paul speaks of *reckoning* faith unto
righteousness, Osiander interprets him as saying that the ungodly are *made* just. When Paul, in Romans 8, says that it
is God who justifies, he contrasts pardon to accusation.
Osiander, however, says that Abraham was accounted as
righteous only after he, embracing Christ, excelled in precious
virtues.

Calvin's dispute with this idea reveals his concern with
sola fide, with the sovereign character of grace. For Calvin
the assurance of salvation was the suckling child of grace.
Faith, while directed to Christ, is not Christ; while directed
to His righteousness, is not His righteousness. To identify
them is to give us a righteousness corollary to that of Christ.
This, says Calvin, "is an impiety not to be tolerated." It tends,
under the pretext of a two-fold righteousness to "weaken the
assurance of salvation and to elevate us above the clouds, that
we may not embrace by faith the grace of expiation, and call
upon God with tranquility of mind."[38]

In both of these disputes — with Rome and with Osiander
— there lies the problem of the analytical and synthetic doctrines of justification, which engaged so much energy and
thought years later. The problem is perhaps not stated as

37. *Ibid.*
38. *Ibid.*, III, xi, 11.

clearly in this form as it could be. But the heart of the matter
is laid bare. The basic issue is whether justification is the
ground of sanctification so that sanctification is continually
rooted in justification, or whether justification itself takes
the form of an infused, sanctifying grace.

That the Reformation, its stress on the imperative of real
conversion and renewal of life notwithstanding, preserved the
forensic nature of justification only underscores how well it
understood justification as the forgiveness of sins. Though
Calvin recognizes that justification and regeneration are inseparable, he insists that the believer is justified in quite
another manner than he is reborn into newness of life. Justification is a sovereign act of God's good mercy. Let it become
involved in the relativity of our human existence and development, and our hearts will be cast into doubt even as the
doctrine of justification itself will be poisoned at its very
roots.[39]

Thus, *sola fide* and *sola gratia* formed the central bulwark
of the Reformation. What is more, they were never separated
from a simple grasp of the gospel of God's grace. Justification,
so understood, was not one specific phase among many on
the way of salvation. It was the sweet word of pardon,
which was and remained of all-embracing significance for
the wholeness of life. Justification may never become a sta-
tion along the way, a harbor which, once passed through, may
be forgotten. On the contrary, only in intimate connection
with justification does talk of sanctification make any real
sense.

The Reformation, in its defense of the forensic, declarative
justification that points us always to the free favor of God,
has not endangered, but rescued the confession of true
sanctification.

---

39. *Ibid,*

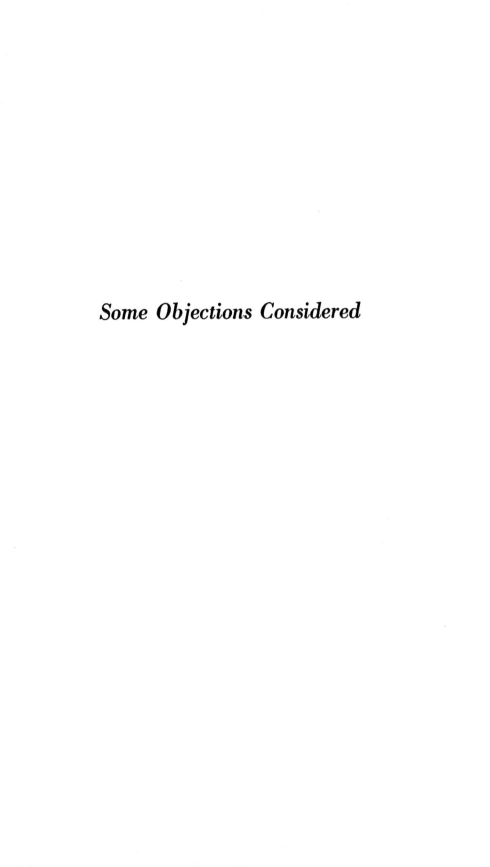

Some Objections Considered

CHAPTER V

Some Objections Considered

IN OUR discussion of the scriptural character of justification by faith alone, we avoided reference to certain important objections that have been leveled against the Reformation *sola fide* doctrine. To these we must turn now. They are significant in that they arise from specific scriptural grounds. Moreover, attention to them promises reward since they touch upon some sensitive points in the relationship between faith and works. We shall weigh the main objections under the following three headings: Judgment according to works; The idea of reward in Scripture; and, Justification according to James.

1. *Judgment according to works.* We need not be astonished that, when we have expressed the Reformed confession of justification, others remind us of the Bible's insistence that *we shall all be judged according to the works done in the flesh.* Such reminders force us to ask ourselves whether the radical *sola fide* doctrine has failed to consider the whole of the multiform preaching of Scripture. For the objection is not based on a few incidental references to the eschatological judgment according to works. Judgment according to works is declared with sharp and sustained accents, and we simply must listen with deep earnestness.

In the first place, this does not suggest a possible cleavage between Paul and the other writers. In Paul, as elsewhere, we are impressed by an unambiguous eschatological perspective of the judgment which shall be according to *works.* Compare, for example, the clarity of his witness to it in Romans

2:6. He signalizes the threat of the day of wrath and the revelation of the righteous judgment of God "who will render to every man according to his works; to them that by patience in well-doing seek for glory and honor and incorruption, eternal life: but unto them that are factious, and obey not the truth, but obey unrighteousness, shall be wrath and indignation" (Rom. 2:6-8).

The relation between final judgment and works is here unmistakably intimate. There is a final divorce between obedience and disobedience. And the question arises whether the intensity of Paul's message of justification, as we saw it in the previous chapter, is not here diverted into a sphere of human morality. Does not Paul descend from the supraethical atmosphere of justification to the mundane area of human decision for good or evil?

The question is the more insistent in view of other utterances of Paul. "Be not deceived; God is not mocked: for whatsoever a man soweth, that shall he also reap. For he that soweth unto his own flesh shall of the flesh reap corruption; but he that soweth unto the Spirit shall of the Spirit reap eternal life. And let us not be weary in well-doing: for in due season we shall reap, if we faint not" (Gal. 6:7-9). "For we must all be made manifest before the judgment-seat of Christ; that each one may receive the things done in the body, according to what he hath done, whether it be good or bad" (II Cor. 5:10). "Whatsoever ye do, work heartily, as unto the Lord, and not unto men; knowing that from the Lord ye shall receive the recompense of the inheritance: ye serve the Lord Christ. For he that doeth wrong shall receive again for the wrong that he hath done: and there is no respect of persons" (Col. 3:23-25). "Each man's work shall be made manifest: for the day shall declare it, because it is revealed in fire; and the fire itself shall prove each man's work of what sort it is" (I Cor. 3:13). And when the Lord comes, he will "bring to light the hidden things of darkness, and make manifest the counsels of the hearts; and then shall each man have his praise from God" (I Cor. 4:5).[1]

We can hardly say that such ideas form a subordinate line, a secondary and rather unimportant element of Paul's message. Quite the contrary. The utmost earnestness of the judgment and the appeal to man to consider his daily responsibility before the Lord of life sound clarionlike through his whole witness. It is not to be denied that for Paul, too, the works and affairs of man play a role in the final drama of God's judgment.

We find the same accents in Peter: "And if ye call on him as Father, who without respect of persons judgeth according to each man's work, pass the time of your sojourning in fear" (I Pet. 1:17). In fact, the same alarming dispatch is spread all through the pages of divine revelation. "Thou renderest to every man according to his work," says the inspired poet (Ps. 62:12). And who could forget the preacher's final thrust: "For God will bring every work into judgment, with every hidden thing, whether it be good, or whether it be evil" (Eccl. 12:14).

It is perhaps of peculiar significance that we find the same theme in the teaching of Jesus. "For the Son of man shall come in the glory of his Father with his angels; and then shall he render unto every man according to his deeds" (Matt. 16:27). The Saviour teaches that the great divorce in the final judgment is tied up with the concrete acts of man during his present life (Matt. 25:31-46). They inherit the Kingdom who gave their brothers — and, in them, Christ — water in their thirst, bread in their hunger, clothes in their nakedness, and friendship in their banishment. They are the justified to whose astonished query shall come to reply: This ye have done unto *Me!* The interdependence between the ultimate judgment and the works of the present life is plain. According

---

1. Cf. also the passage about the ministers of Satan, whose end shall be according to their works (II Cor. 11:15).

to the Lord, we shall be judged on the broad expanse of our entire lives and on every chance word spoken in an idle moment (Matt. 12:36). And to all this, Christ adds: "For by thy word thou shalt be justified, and by thy words thou shalt be condemned" (Matt. 12:37).[2]

The only norm, it would seem, is that of *actuality*. There is no more room, apparently, for a supra-ethical judgment than for a judgment based on race or color, on a respect for persons. The divine judgment comes on the heels of the actuality of this life as God Himself discerns it. In contrast to a "respect of persons" stands the judgment according to works. The word *analytical* is the one word qualified to describe this situation; the word *synthetic* is ruled out. Does not this, then, create a profound, inner contradiction within the witness of Scripture, even within the circle of Paul's own letters? Does not the doctrine of forensic justification, synthetic and declarative as it is, impugn and antagonize this divine analysis, this analytic basis for His final Word? In brief, how can we conciliate the biblical norm of morality for the final judgment with Paul's message of justification without the works of the law?

This question was occasion for Lietzmann to write: "In verses 5 to 12 [of Romans 2] Paul argues from the pre-gospel standpoint which knew no faith-righteousness and expected a judgment on the ground of individual accomplishments."[3] Is it, thus, true that two lines cross here, the vertical line of justification by faith and the horizontal line of morals and work-righteousness? Is *sola fide* an isolated notion "from beyond good and evil" somehow smuggled into the faithful witness of a judgment according to works? *Sola fide* has to do with a merciful divine judgment of the *ungodly*, of *sinners* and *publicans* who enter ahead of the moral Pharisees into

---

2. Jesus uses the same word for justify here as Paul does in Romans.
3. H. Lietzmann, *An die Römer* in *Handbuch zum N. T.*, 1933, p. 39.

the Kingdom of God; this turns the judgment according to works upside down.

On the other hand, if, as has been said, election lies at the heart of the Church, is not the judgment according to works a "foreign body" in her doctrine? And if election means, according to the scriptural description of the state of Jacob and Esau, that the greater shall serve the lesser (Rom. 9:11, 12) — a description that applies to the yet unborn who, naturally, had done neither good nor evil — how can the eschatological warnings be ethically defined?

Reflection, however, suggests not two opposing lines of argument, but a profound harmony within the witness of Scripture on this point. We do not read in Scripture a series of isolated utterances on faith-righteousness and then again another series, equally isolated, on judgment according to works. The mere fact that Paul speaks so often and so fervently about justification by faith and equally often and fervently about judgment according to works should lead us to expect a dove-tailing between them. Graffman writes: "It is only at first blush that Paul, in his many expostulations concerning judgment, seems to overlook the distinctive role of faith."[4] Paul does indeed set the righteousness of faith in contradiction to the righteousness of works — he could not have done it more definitely — yet he urges the necessity of works. The works he wants, however, are not the works of the law. These works are in close affinity with and are, in fact, embraced by faith-righteousness.

When Paul, in Romans 12, prays the brothers to present their bodies as a living, holy, and reasonable sacrifice to God, and continually appeals to the church for concrete acts of love, he is not thinking in an ethical channel isolated from the main arteries of the gospel. Nor does he try to graft a moralism to the main trunk of grace. Paul warns and appeals "by

---

4. H. Graffmann, "Das Gericht nach den Werken in Matthäusevangelium," in *Theologische Aufsätze Karl Barth zum 50. Geburtstag, 1936,* p. 131.

the mercy of God" (Rom. 12:1 ff.). These words do not form an ill-considered, traditional exhortative cliché. They are the only possible and only real basis of the meaningful and forceful monition of Romans 12. The concrete deeds of brotherly love, joy, patience, hospitality, single-mindedness, humility, and love of enemies are set, for Paul, in the stream of God's commiseration. Without that gracious cleansing they change color and character. Paul's eye is on the work of faith and the toil of love in the sense in which he portrays the Thessalonians (I Thess. 1:3). There is no dualism between faith and these works, though there is a dualism here and everywhere between faith and the works of the law. The relation between faith and works is so intimate that Paul can say that all which is not of faith is sin (Rom. 14:23).

With this marriage of faith and works in view, it is clear that all works done in this life are subjected to God's judgment, and that everything hinges on whether they are done in faith. The human situation is not a contest between fruitless faith and moral striving; it is defined by the distinction between the "works of faith" and the "works of the law." The line separating these is sharp and has eschatological relevance. Faith is not a given, a datum external to concrete human life. Paul knows of a calling to freedom and a service in love (Gal. 5:13); he knows that a Christian must walk through the Holy Spirit, bearing His fruit: love, joy, peace, longsuffering, kindness, goodness, faithfulness, meekness, self-control (Gal. 5:22, 23).

Sola fide does not make real life unimportant. In Romans and in Galatians, where justification apart from the works of the law is maintained so stoutly, we are urged to walk in the Spirit. This suggests, not a contradiction in Paul's thought, but the existential character of faith, of this faith which is not a subjective human attitude, but a confident repose in God's pity and grace! Thus faith is here decisive for awful consequences. For, without pretension or conceit, it expects everything from grace. It does not create a field along-side of itself for moral exercise. It *defines* life, not merely as a dynamic force with a discrete causality, but as trust in God's mercy and as a "therefore stand" in freedom.

Peter also speaks of the significance of works in connection with his preaching of redemption through the precious blood of Christ (I Pet. 1:17, 19). Precisely because it is not a tenuous function of thought, but a gravitation toward an object (and what an object!), this faith is concrete. "The doing of the will of God is proof of whether faith is true faith or empty acknowledgment and conviction, mere feeling and experience, vain repetition of *Yea, Yea,* or *Lord! Lord!*"[5]

Though it is difficult to characterize this relationship be-tween faith and works precisely, we may speak of works as *giving form to* faith. To *this* faith. Barth has called it the "lived-out reality" of faith. And certainly the works of faith get their importance from *sola fide,* since faith embraces Christ and the believer is Christ's own possession. The tree, according to Jesus, is known by its fruit (Matt. 12:33), and faith is known by its works. The works of the law and these works of faith have really nothing in common. It is remark-able that the "justified" of Matthew 25 ask in *amazement,* "Lord, when did we see thee hungry and feed thee, or thirsty and gave thee to drink? And when have we seen you a stranger and took thee in, or naked and clothed thee?" The questions suggest a forgetfulness of good works, and the answer says that, at bottom, what was done for the miserable and destitute was a deed done to *Christ.*

There is nothing to be seen of a self-sufficient ethic. And since the intimacy between faith and grace, between faith and its possession, forms the background of all warnings and ex-hortation, the judgment according to works is, in the most profound sense, a judgment concerning faith and unbelief. This is always the measuring rod in the judgment according

---

5. *Ibid.,* p. 132.

to works. Christ speaks of the hypocrites of whom Isaiah prophesied: "This people honoreth me with their lips; but their heart is far from me" (Matt. 15:7). The *words* of the people are put under the critical norm of Him who knows the inner recesses of the heart. "In the final analysis, works as such never determine the sentence."[6] Although the works do determine the sentence in one sense, they never do so in their phenomenological, neutral observability (the casting out of devils, for instance). It is only in their divinely recognized quality as defined by faith, that is to say, as they are conditioned by Christ and His salvation. Judgment according to works, then, is not an analytical ethical judgment, but an infallible perception of works in their relation to faith. Recall the definition of good works in the Heidelberg Catechism, where only those works are called good which rise from a true faith and aim at the honor of God.[7]

What Christ said to the woman in Simon's house in Bethany as she anointed His head with precious oil, applies to every good work that shall withstand the fire of judgment: "She hath wrought a good work *on Me*" (Matt. 26:10). The relation between faith and work is no less evident in the connection between being pardoned and being ready to pardon. The correlation is so close that we read: "For if ye forgive men their trespasses, your heavenly Father will also forgive you. But if ye forgive not men their trespasses, neither will your Father forgive your trespasses" (Matt. 6:14, 15). In the parable of the unjust steward this correlation is revealed especially in this, that the steward (whose debt of 10,000 talents had been erased) had his debt recharged to him because he refused to remit the trivial debt of another (Matt. 18:23-25). The plea for mercy (Matt. 18:26, 29) was heard in the first instance, denied in the second. The merciless creditor appealed to the mercy he never understood and, in

6. *Ibid.*, p. 131.
7. Heidelberg Catechism, Lord's Day 32.

the end, it profited him nothing. The Heidelberg Catechism has a beautiful statement in reference to the fifth petition of the Lord's Prayer about the witness of God's grace in us to the effect that our life's intent is to forgive our neighbor with our whole heart.[8]

The disposition to forgive is not simply a general characteristic of moral virtue; it is embodied only in a self-humiliation before divine grace. This is why this disposition is a witness to God's grace and, embodied in the great act of forgiveness (the talents), is of eschatological decisiveness. This is also why the works of the law and the works of faith are as removed from each other as East is from West. The most impressive works, such as prophecy and casting out of devils in the name of Christ, are no guarantee against the judgment and no security that the prophets and miracle workers are not actually workers of unrighteousness (cf. Matt. 7:22; Luke 13:25, 26).

The correlation of faith and works is made clear in many ways. The parable of the two sons evidently has to do with concrete acts of obedience, with doing the will of the Father (Matt. 21:28, 31). But in the application of the parable, Christ makes the charge that his listeners, in contrast to the publicans and harlots, never really believed John. They never repented that they might believe (Matt. 21:32). In the lesson about the expectation of the coming Lord, it is the evil servant who says, "My Lord tarrieth." And his works are in keeping with his lack of confidence. The faithful and wise servant, however, is keyed to the coming of his Lord and keeps watch over the house in expectation (Matt. 24:43-51).

The biblical picture of the judgment according to works never indicates the existence of an alternative way of salvation, another way than *sola fide*. The payment on the basis of works is definitely in conflict with all antinomianism, but not at all with justification by faith. To suggest such conflict

---

8. *Ibid.*, Question 126.

or to read two mutually limiting or two complementing thoughts into Paul, is to reduce the works of faith to an autonomous ethic, to negate any thorough criticism of the idea that justification is achieved through the merit of good works, or, to put it so, to devaluate works of faith to the level of works of the law.

It is the works of the law, not those of faith, which threaten *sola fide*. We shall all stand before the judgment seat of Christ, and there everything done in darkness shall be brought into the light (II Cor. 5:10; I Cor. 4:4, 5). He is the Judge, of whom the Credo confesses that He shall come to judge the living and the dead. But this Judge is the Mediator between God and man. God shall judge righteously in Him (Acts 17:31). And in Him, as Judge, lies the perfect, finished concord between *sola fide* and the judgment according to works. The Church awaits in this Judge the same One who once before, for my sake, put Himself under God's judgment and removed all condemnation from me.[9] It is He whom we anticipate in the judgment — the just judgment according to works. And only thus, in the message of Christ's second coming, are we comforted and do we take heart, looking for that day with great expectations.[10]

*   *   *

2. *The idea of reward in Scripture.* In so far as the notion of reward in Scripture is engaged as an argument against *sola fide*, it is directly related to the preceding discussion of the judgment according to works. It is, we may presume, natural that this objection, too, should be raised against the confession of justification by faith. For here, as in the case of the divine judgment, a certain tension is at first apparent between the idea of reward and that of unmerited acceptance by God. A divine reward would seem to correspond to cer-

---

9. Cf. Heidelberg Catechism, Question 52.
10. Cf. Belgic Confession, Art. 37.

tain human feats. Can it then be possible to let the Scripture freely speak its message regarding divine rewards without concluding that human works have, in some sense at least, a token of genuine merit?

* * *

Reformed theology is not infrequently charged by Roman theologians with having taken the props from under the scriptural teaching of divine rewards. Even Abraham Kuyper felt that the question of reward "has without doubt been neglected much too long by Reformed writers and preachers."[11] Motivated by fear of the meritoriousness of good works, the promised rewards are "suffered to lie in death-like silence, whereby the goad to piety, given by the Scriptures in the form of the rich and many-faceted promise of reward, is blunted."[12] Whether this remark about Reformed writers is justified or not, it is quite to the point to say that our controversy with Rome should not limit our own perspectives. We have reason to be thankful that our confessions do not hesitate to speak freely about the promised rewards.[13]

The witness of the Scriptures is too insistent for the message concerning our promised reward to be neglected for any length of time. Barth has said that Luther preached too persistently about that which is now once and for all established and waiting only to be made known, but we need not enter on that. Calvin, however, did speak extensively over rewards, though most of his discussion wore an antithetical garb — that it is impermissible to conclude justification by works from the promise of rewards.[14] This antithesis does not stem from mere reaction, for it was vitally necessary for him to set up barriers against an attack on the harmonious testimony of Scripture to the all-sufficiency of grace.

11. A. Kuyper, *E Voto*, II, p. 377.
12. *Ibid.*
13. Cf. Heidelberg Catechism, Question 63; Belgic Confession, Art. 34.
14. Calvin, *Institutes*, III. xviii.

The divine promise of reward — reward given to all who walk in His ways — is recorded in many passages of Scripture. The idea of reward is confirmed in the Bible as an integral element in the preaching of the gospel. Reward is often spoken of in the Old Testament, though not always in that specific terminology. Certainly Proverbs is the most eloquent spokesman. "The doings of a man's hands shall be rendered unto him" (Prov. 12:14). "He that feareth the commandment shall be rewarded" (Prov. 13:13). The Lord makes rich (Prov. 10:22) and lengthens the days of man. The way of the Lord is strength to the upright (Prov. 10:27, 29) and the righteous shall never be moved (Prov. 10:30). "The hoary head is a crown of glory. It shall be found in the way of righteousness" (Prov. 16:31). "He who keepeth the commandment keepeth his soul" (Prov. 19:16). The blessing of the Lord rests on the children of those who walk in integrity (Prov. 20:7). He who heeds instruction is on the way of life (Prov. 10:17). The path of the ungodly is a dead-end; the life of the righteous is the way of light. "For surely there is a reward" and you who live in the fear of the Lord shall not have your hope cut off (Prov. 23:18). In all sorts of ordinary circumstances of life a reward is held in sight. "If thine enemy be hungry, give him bread to eat; and if he be thirsty, give him water to drink: For thou wilt heap coals of fire on his head, and Jehovah will reward thee" (Prov. 25:21, 22). There are manifold blessings for those who live in fear of the Lord (Prov. 10:6).

The Psalms present the same picture. It is the comfort of Israel that "the eye of Jehovah is upon them that fear Him, . . . to deliver their soul from death, and to keep them alive in famine (Ps. 33:18, 19). An answer rings out to the cry of the righteous, and there is a comforting correlation between the walk in His fear and the divine answer for today and the future (cf. Ps. 34:37; Ps. 84:12, 13; Ps. 94:14; Ps. 146). This connection may be summarized: "Commit thy way unto Jehovah. Trust also in Him . . . He will make thy righteousness to go forth as the light, and thy justice as the noonday" (Ps. 37:5, 6).

There is, obviously, no polite moralism in all this, no neat correspondence of the "good life" with the successful life. The religious overtones are too evident here, even though they may at times be in the background; there is too much of trust in and prayer to the God of the Covenant to allow for such a humanly construed correlation. There is a correspondence, and a concrete one, but it is built on the pillars of religion, of love and hate, as already established in the Torah: "I Jehovah thy God am a jealous God, visiting the iniquity . . . upon the third and upon the fourth generation of them that hate me, and showing lovingkindness unto thousands of them that love me and keep my commandments" (Ex. 20:5, 6).

Nevertheless, there is a divine act in the life of the righteous — those who fear and trust Jehovah — which corresponds, not *per se*, but in grace, to their fear of the Lord and their life in that fear. This is hardly to be gainsaid (cf. Is. 26:7).

In the New Testament, too, this correspondence is omnipresent. We may recall the advice to lay up treasures in heaven (Matt. 6:20). The mere forms of good works are continually exposed as sham, works such as loving those who love us (Matt. 6:1, 2, 16), or fasting and charity done for people to see. For this there is only a knife-edged warning: "Verily, verily, I say unto you, they have received their reward." That is to say, they have no reward with the Father in Heaven for they have had their reward already. They have received it where they sought it, among men. According to the correspondence between the deeds and human rewards, they have had theirs, and have lost the real divine reward.[15]

15. The Greek word is *apechein*, meaning they have had their reward in full. The idea seems to be that they have already received their stipulation, and can make no further claims for payment.

Despite the strength of the warning here against miscalculating the rewards coming to us, there is implicit in the very warning against this sort of lust for human recognition a suggestion of the way in which one does receive a reward — not immediately, but in the future and from the Father Himself. Thus, Jesus concludes His beatitudes with: "Rejoice, and be exceeding glad; for great is your reward in heaven" (Matt. 5:12). In contrast to the charity of those hungry for the word of praise is the alms-giving of those whose left hand does not know what the right hand is doing (Matt. 6:3). To these it is said: "Thy Father, who seeth in secret shall reward thee" (Matt. 6:4).

Everywhere in the New Testament this remarkable parallel appears: "And judge not, and ye shall not be judged: and condemn not, and ye shall not be condemned: release, and ye shall be released: give, and it shall be given unto you; good measure, pressed down, shaken together, running over, shall they give unto your bosom. For with what measure ye mete it shall be measured to you again" (Luke 6:37, 38).

There is a balance between giving and receiving, an appropriate reward for each of various deeds. It has been so expressed that man receives a reward "where such obedience is performed pre-eminently,"[16] that is, when he responds "extraordinarily and unprecedentedly to love." This can be seen in Luke 6, where it is not to love, to lend money, to do favors in response to such favors from others, that is praised. Sinners do that much. Their works of charity are reactions to the stimulus of charity extended to themselves. They arise from sheer egotism. They take their respectable place in the self-centeredness of the average life in which one's fellow is the means toward the richer cultivation of one's own existence. Who does no more must take his place among the sinners. We can agree that reward is given only to those who do "extraordinary" charity, provided that it is not the brilliant, the

---

16. Kittel, *Theologisches Wörterbuch zum N. T.*, IV, *misthos*, p. 703.

sensational, the striking in the sense that we usually think of as *extraordinary*. It must be a strike, a thrust through, to beyond the *realm* of "ordinary" charity. Thus, in Luke 6:35, it is the "extraordinary" love toward an enemy which pierces the barrier of the "ordinary" correspondence of the getting and giving of love. For this "extraordinary," this "abnormal" love the reward shall be large, and the lover shall be a son of the Most High, "for he is kind toward the unthankful and evil" (Luke 6:35).

There is, thus, no simple, well-balanced, self-regulating correlation between work and reward. A correlation is present, however, and Jesus uses it in his teaching as a stimulant and warning. It forms an integral part of the scriptural message; it is not hid from us now to be sprung on us later as a divine surprise. For this reason, it merits our study. The Bible apparently is not cramped by fear of clouding up the purity of the ethical life. The problem hinted at here is well enough known: everything ethical is viewed askance whenever it presumes to influence our affairs with the enticement of reward or payment; there can be a pure ethical transaction only when all consideration of reward is disregarded.

An extreme example of this is the contention that pure ethical conduct is only possible by means of an atheistic ethic in which good is done only for the sake of the good, with no consideration of reward for the doing of it. Only thus would the absoluteness of moral life be safeguarded against utilitarianism, pragmatism, and eudaemonism. "Not only rewards and punishment, but the entire consideration of the ethical life on the basis of a holy, living, divine will collapses from this point of view."[17] Troeltsch, who generally rejects it, says also of this ethic that "it makes, or can make, a profound moral impression on the conscience,"[18] but that it does this by means of a certain "enchantment of honesty and resigna-

---

17. E. Troeltsch, *Atheistische Ethik*, Vol. II of *Gesammelte Schriften*, 1922, p. 533.
18. *Ibid.*, p. 546.

tion." By forgetting the possibility of reward, man honors the ethical norm in its categorical purity. The motive for good works is not sought for anywhere but in the moral imperative itself. Only in this self-less manner can the demon ego be crushed, and the heart cleared for pure intentions, for a true altruism that seeks only the good of the other.[19] This is the "noble" ethic of the godless.

The Word of God takes quite another attitude than such "pure-ethical" views.[20] It is hardly naive as to the radical corruption and egoism of man. Nor is it of a mind to say that all connection between human works and proffered reward necessarily feeds and quicken egoism. The morality of the Bible is in this sense an offense to the teachers of the "purely moral." It admonishes us not to lose sight of the promised boon. "Whatsoever ye do," says Paul, "work heartily, as unto the Lord, and not unto men; knowing that from the Lord ye shall receive the recompense of the inheritance" (Col. 3:23, 24). A crown of righteousness awaits Paul, he testifies, and all others, too, who love His appearing (II Tim. 4:8). He is the just Judge; therefore take heart "for God is not unrighteous to forget your work and the love which ye showed toward his name, in that ye ministered unto the saints, and still do minister" (Heb. 6:10). When Hebrews tells how Moses chose to endure the burdens of his people and the people of God rather than fatten in the gardens of Egypt's royal house, considering the reproach of Christ finer stuff than the wealth of Pharaoh, it adds: "for he looked unto the recompense of great reward" (Heb. 11:26). This is hardly the cold purity of an unmotivated ethic. Reward in this decisive choice of Moses is suggested as a legitimate and praiseworthy motivation. Though we open

---

19. *Ibid.*, p. 546.
20. Cf. Abraham Kuyper's remarks about the "spiritual souls" who present themselves as being too big to be motivated by reward. Kuyper calls these "too spiritual people" back to obedience to the Word, which, after all, knows better than they "what is needful for their nature, their position in the kingdom, and their stimulation to zeal." *E Voto*, II, p. 384.

ourselves to misunderstanding, we can hardly disagree with
Barth when he says that the statement "Faith works for this
reward" is not a Roman Catholic, but a Christian statement.
We often say that what we are really concerned about is not
the reward that may come to us. What we ought to mean by
this is simply that religion is not a sop to our egoism and a
cloak for avariciousness. There is a scriptural way, a third
way, between an eudaemonistic ethic and a formal, categorical
ethic of sheer duty. And with this we must state our question: how are we to construe unity between the radical
biblical doctrine of *sola fide* and the scriptural promise of
payment of rewards?[21]

* * *

We shall first consider, profitably I think, Abraham
Kuyper's rather unique understanding of rewards.[22] He
makes a distinction between eternal life as such and a special
honor or pleasure in eternal life. Eternal life is won by
Christ for all the redeemed; but for some redeemed there is
a reward of grace over and above this. The reward of grace,
argues Kuyper, can hardly be the same as the eternal life
given to the entire host of redeemed souls. It must be a
special gift, something additional. We find this in his reading of the passage regarding the laying up of treasures. That
which we should lay up in heaven is this special gift, this
reward which is in the nature of recompense. Through suffering and cross-bearing on earth a capacity for greater bliss
can be created in the soul; and God promises that, as reward,
the soul will be filled with felicity to that capacity. This
greater happiness, directly related to our life on earth, though
given in God's free grace, is the crown in heaven to which
the Saviour refers in the Sermon on the Mount. We must
all appear before the judgment seat of Christ, there to have

21. Cf. also Rev. 20:12; Rev. 22:12; Rev. 11:17, 18; I Cor. 3:8; Heb.
10:35; Heb. 11:6.
22. For this discussion of Kuyper see *E Voto*, II, pp. 384-395.

exposed everything we have done in this life for evil or good. Then comes the reward "which God shall mete out to each of the redeemed who, through prayers and charity, through self-denial and the joyful bearing of his cross, has laid away a treasure in heaven."

Kuyper illustrates all this with the "extra gift" that parents present to their children as an unexpected surprise, something to which the children had no claim or right. If there were any claim or right to it, this reward would be degraded to a payment. In this way, Kuyper seeks to follow the line taken by the catechism that reward is given, not of merit, but of grace.[23]

But Kuyper's interesting ideas must be put to the test of Scripture. He himself admitted it was difficult to maintain his distinction between eternal life and reward when he faced the words of Christ: "And every one that hath left houses or brethren, or sisters, or father, or mother, or children, or lands, for my name's sake, shall receive a hundredfold, and shall inherit eternal life" (Matt. 19:29). For here the special gift is mentioned in the same breath as eternal life, both in correspondence to self-sacrifice for Christ's sake. Kuyper argued that this cannot mean that eternal life itself is a reward of grace for bearing the cross, since in Scripture generally, it is "not the cross that the Christian bears in following Christ, but the cross which Christ bore which is the basis for eternal life.[24] He understands Christ's statement, then, as saying that, in addition to the inheritance of eternal life, which is every believer's certainty, a reward of grace is also held out.

The reader perhaps already feels that Kuyper's characterization of reward is incapable of scriptural defense. It is not surprising either that other Reformed theologians fail to come to Kuyper's conclusions.[25] The text from Matthew 19

---

23. Heidelberg Catechism, Lord's Day 24.
24. Kuyper, E Voto, II, p. 385.
25. Cf. Calvin, Institutes, III, xviii, 3, where he speaks of eternal life as the reward for works.

cited above already suggests another approach. Kuyper's manipulation of this text fails to satisfy. It is quite true that Christ's cross and not ours earns eternal life for us. But this suggests that our works do earn us something of a special recompense of grace beyond eternal life. And this is hardly the argument of Scripture. All heavenly rewards flow to us from the merits of our crucified Saviour. Undeniably, Christ counts eternal life as a reward which they receive who have left all to follow Christ. Ridderbos claims that the accent in Matthew 19 is put especially on this point — that they shall inherit eternal life. "In this for the first time the real position of the children of God and the blessed of the Father shall be revealed, and they shall receive a hundred-fold, as an incorruptible and eternal possession, for what they lost in this life."[26]

If we were to distinguish eternal life from special rewards, we would be forced to contend that the earning of rewards has an independent significance side by side with the merits of Christ.[27] This is not to deny that Scripture often speaks of variations and gradations in the Kingdom of Glory, nor that all this bears upon the idea of rewards. Bavinck says that differing levels of glory are taught by Scripture especially where the rewards which each shall receive according to his works are under consideration.[28] But how are we to understand this correlation between rewards and man's life and work on earth? The question has grown in importance since Rome developed her doctrine of the merit of good works on the foundation of the doctrine of rewards. To speak the truth we must insist that on one hand the correspondence between

26. H. N. Ridderbos *Mattheüs*, II, in the *Korte Verklaring*, p. 68. Cf. also F. W. Grosheide, *Commentaar op Mattheüs*, p. 233: "Eternal life awaits as an inheritance, that is to say, as something good that now lies prepared and which they shall certainly receive. . . . This is the completeness of the reward. . ."
27. This was not Kuyper's intent, of course, but his argument necessarily suggests it.
28. H. Bavinck. *Gereformeerde Dogmatik*, IV, p. 711.

work and reward must be maintained, while on the other that every merit that could accrue to good works be denied. According to Rome this is a paradoxical, self-contradictory solution. According to the Reformed confessions it is the only way to understand scriptural preaching in its wholeness. Perhaps if we reflect somewhat further, we can at least make this solution meaningful for our faith.

* * *

The first text that comes to mind, perhaps, is Romans 4:4: "Now to him that worketh, the reward is not reckoned as of grace, but as of debt."[29]   Paul is at work here unfolding the radical antithesis between justification according to the works of the law and justification by faith. He points out that the "worker" receives his compensation, not out of grace, but according to what is owed him. There is, then, a correlation between work and payment — a contractual agreement, into which grace does not enter because it is merit and achievement which determines the correlation. It is the same as with work and wages in everyday economic agreements. Scripture suggests this with its reminder that the worker has his pay coming to him (cf. Luke 10:7) and when Old and New Testament insist that the laborer, on the grounds of his work done, has a just claim to the fruits of his labor (cf. Lev. 19:13; Deut. 24:13; James 5:4). Achievement is here the obvious determinative of the relation between work and reward. With the same principle in mind, Scripture speaks as well about the reward of the unrighteous, meaning that the works done in unrighteousness is the basis for its own appropriate reward (cf. Acts 1:18; II Pet. 2:13; Jude 11).

The idea of reward on the basis of works suggests its own contrast, *the reward based on grace.* This phrase has been

---

29. Lietzmann writes that if he had been concerned with logical sentence structure, Paul would have had to continue: "To him, however, that worketh not and yet receives a reward, it is reckoned not as of works but as of grace." *An die Römer,* in *Hanbuch zum N. T.,* 1933, p. 53.

called, not incorrectly, "a unique combination." Since the catechism radically repudiates the Judaistic notion of reward as a compensation for achievement, it could be expected to disclaim *ipso facto* every idea of reward. This is however not the case.

The sense of the scriptural presentation of rewards has been approached in many ways, some more successful than others. Michel talks about a "purification of the idea of rewards,"[30] meaning thereby that we should rid the idea of every vestige of achievement. It is questionable whether it is proper to speak of a purification at this point. We are more concerned with getting at the pith of the idea of rewards within the all determinative grace of God. The element of prestige is, indeed, excluded in the sense of a worker demanding his recompense as his right. Reward is not a contractual answer to an earned claim. The correlation of work and reward in the relationship of sinner to God takes on quite another character than it has in an industrial contract.

At the time of the Reformation, and later in the Reformed confessions, a verse in Luke 17 received a good deal of attention: "Even so ye also, when ye shall have done all the things that are commanded you, say, We are unprofitable servants: we have done that which it was our duty to do" (Luke 17:10). The verses leading up to this one, which was cited so often, especially in Lutheran theology, are concerned with the Lord of the workers who, when the workers had performed their duties, gave them no thanks. Since Jesus uses the servant-master relationship here, He evidently seeks to underscore the repudiation of merit. Even with the complete performance of the obligation, there is no room for self-congratulation. Whether the believer is actually in state to perform this, is another question. Here the point is that we are unprofitable servants. This sentence so patently excludes

---

30. O. Michel, "Der Lohngedanke in der Verkündigung Jesu," in *Zeitung für Systematische Theologie*, 1932, p. 51.

every possible notion of merit and claim, that one is amazed that Rome has not been better able to understand and emulate the Reformation recollection of it.

But Rome continues to insist heartily on the meritorious-ness of good works. Yet, Roman Catholic theologians, too, must do something with Romans 4:4. It is understood, of course, that Paul rejects works, in so far as they are works for reward according to merit, works of the law through which no justification is possible. Therefore Roman thinkers try to devest the meritoriousness of good works of grounds for self-congratulation by teaching the presence of grace *in* the meriting. The merit of good works and the claim upon reward entailed in it, however, remains and dominates in spite of the admission of grace into the process. The Roman doctrine of merit, all casuistry notwithstanding, comes to the same thing as the Judaistic hope of "reward according to rights." It was this which the reformers threw off with all their souls' strength, for they had learned to read Paul again, and there the message was plain — reward is of grace. In the Roman view the idea of reward based on merit is maintained, and, accordingly, with Rome, the reward cannot be founded upon grace.

The parable of the workers in the vineyard sheds much light on our question (Matt. 20:1-16). Parables must be approached carefully; one is tempted to wring too much from them in order to prove or illustrate a point. This particular parable does not present a systematic argument concerning the relation of worker to his pay. It is, to be sure, a picture out of ordinary life, a labor situation which is regulated according to contractual agreement. But to this is added the liberal attitude of the employer in taking on the last-minute workers and paying them the full day's wages. These had not shared with the others the full day's sweat and toil under the scorching sun. Accordingly, the first workers neither understood nor accepted the sovereign liberality[31] of the employer, for his generosity broke through the normal construction of merit and reward. Considered from within their own perspective, they were dead right. Such generosity has no place and cannot be meaningfully admitted within a system of strict justice and merit. The element of wonder is excluded from the contractual system. There are no possible surprises in it. But in the act of God, the overflowing generosity of His grace is the great surprise.

The Reformation, we may say, was founded on astonishment at God's goodness. This is why the reformers rejected the Roman theme of the merits of good works in spite of its countermelody of grace. They kept hearing the word *prestige* in the great Tridentine dissertation on merit. It all suggested that a man could stake a claim in the area of salvation. The reformers were not prepared, even in the relation between work and reward, to let go of the fact that the whole of life, its activities and their consequences, flowed out of God's commiseration. Nor would they let go their hold on the truth that this divine mercy was not set in motion by our achievements. Thus, they could not forget the words spoken to the unworthy servants, for we are, as the Belgic Confession says, unable to do any work that is not polluted by our flesh and worthy of condemnation.[32]

Rome, on the other hand, has defended with vigor the thesis that good works have merit before God, and Trent has tried hard to substantiate it.[33] Merit is viewed as "an achievement on behalf of another, through which man therewith earns a claim to recompense."[34] There is an element of a "claim of

---

31. "It is a striking picture of the divine generosity which gives without regard to the measures of strict justice." C. H. Dodd, *The Parables of the Kingdom*, 1936, p. 122.

32. Belgic Confession, Art. 24.

33. Council of Trent, Session VI, Chap. 16 and Canon 32.

34. F. Diekamp, *Katholische Dogmatik nach den Grundsätzen des heiligen Thomas*, 7th ed., 1936, II, p. 539.

law" in this, on the basis of which the contractor has the duty to pay the wage.[35]

The reformers saw clearly that the Roman Catholic Church had forced this notion of merit into the doctrine of grace. Trent had said of works by which man won merit, that one performed them through grace. Later, under the influence of the Reformation, the element of grace was pushed more strongly.[36] In spite of all this, the reformers were not willing to make a single concession. Nor shall we. For the biblical teaching about rewards and the Roman concept of merit are not identical; they are, in fact, in opposition. Let it be said that more recent Roman Catholic theologians have a certain feeling for "dangers concealed within the concept of merit"[37]; but they cannot cast off this concept without throwing out the entire Roman doctrine of grace, a doctrine built out of Rome's synthesis between grace and freedom. This accounts for the fact that the idea of merit and compensation always carries overtones of "pretence" and "claim." And these, in turn, pose a perpetual threat to the doctrine of justification. The protest of the Reformation was not aimed simply at the relation between work and reward, but at the kind of relationship which renders impossible an absolutely pretentionless stance beneath God's mercy and forgiveness. As soon as merit began to suggest that God had an obligation to deliver compensation for human claims, such a stance became less and less possible.

The Roman Catholic doctrine of reward is, thus, identical with its doctrine of works and merit.[38] God becomes indebted to man. This would be unthinkable, according to Diekamp, "without God having through His own ordinance, made Him-

35. *Ibid.*
36. Paul Althaus cites the dogmatics of the Roman Catholic Schmaus who says of merit that "it is grounded finally in divine mercy." Vid. *Die Christliche Wahrheit* in *Lehrbuch der Dogmatik*, II, 1948, p. 467.
37. Althaus, *op. cit.*, p. 468.
38. Cf. Diekamp, *op. cit.*, p. 542. "Rewards, according to Holy Scripture, are established upon the merit of good works."

self a debtor."[39] It was this thought, and the realization that such an understanding of the work-reward relationship was part of the warp and woof of Roman Catholic theology, that ruled out any possibility of compromise for the reformers.

* * *

The relation of father and child may also offer suggestions of the true relation between work and reward. We can take our cue from Calvin, who writes that the kingdom of heaven is not "a stipend to servants, but an inheritance to children." He recalls the promise given to Abraham of seed as numerous as the sands of the sea. And when Abraham showed his readiness to offer Isaac, the son of God's promise, God said again that He would bless him with seed alike in number to the stars in the heavens and the sand on the shores. Are we to conclude, asks Calvin, that Abraham earned that blessing through his obedience? How could he have when the promise was given to him long before the command to offer his son? "Here, then, it appears beyond all doubt that the Lord rewards the works of believers with those blessings which he had already given them before their works were thought of, and while he had no reason for his beneficence but his own mercy."[40]

Calvin's remarks direct us to a correct understanding of the promise of rewards. Rewards have no function which can be isolated from God's mercy. They are, indeed, sealed within this divine clemency. When Calvin is asked what sense talk of reward can have in a case where it has already been promised out of pure mercy, he answers that God wills that we be engaged in good works and aspire to the enjoyment of the reward which he has promised. God's mercy leads His children in safe conduct along the way of salvation on which the reward is held out. It is with justice that Hauck

---

39. *Ibid.*, p. 551.
40. Calvin, *Institutes*, III, xviii, 2.

has spoken of "Calvin's energetic rejection of the causal connection between human merit and divine reward."[41] Calvin sees the matter consistently from the viewpoint of his confession of divine mercy, and expresses it as follows: "Only let us not imagine a reciprocal relation of merit and reward which is the error into which the sophists fell, for want of considering the end which we have stated. . . . Nothing is clearer, than that the promise of a reward to good works is designed to afford some consolation to the weakness of our flesh, but not to inflate our minds with vain-glory. Whoever, therefore, infers from this, that there is any merit in works, or balances the work against the reward, errs very widely from the true design of God."[42]

God the just Judge shall present the crown of righteousness, but, as Calvin concludes from Augustine, the Judge would never present the crown had not the merciful Father given grace.[43] How could God consider anyone worthy of reward "unless his infinite goodness had abolished all their demerit of punishment?" Good works have a part in obtaining a reward only through "their acceptance by the divine mercy."[44] He who concerns himself with the relation between works and reward must keep a steady bearing on God's mercy. Otherwise he will lose himself in a maze of legalism and work-righteousness.

Rewards do not enter as something new side by side with divine mercy. It is only through God's mercy[45] that rewards

41. W. A. Hauck, *Calvin und die Rechtfertigung*, 1938, p. 77.

42. *Institutes*, III, xviii, 4.

43. *Ibid.*, 5.

44. *Ibid.*

45. "And we should always remember that this promise, as well as all others, would be fraught with no benefit to us, unless it were preceded by the gratuitous covenant of mercy, on which the whole certainty of our salvation must depend." *Institutes*, III, xviii, 7.

make any sense.   In the promise of reward is set a goad toward confidence in God's mercy.[46]

It is no accident that Calvin discusses and rejects the Roman premise that we are justified more by love than by faith in the same chapter in which he speaks of the reward of grace.[47] The Reformed mind on the idea of reward touches here the central confession of *sola fide*, a confession which stretches its rays of light over the whole field of Christian doctrine. The confession of God's mercy is so broad and profound that it does not cramp the Christian's hope for reward; it establishes it and gives it meaning.   Rewards and *sola fide-sola gratia* go well together.   It is he who has understood the significance of *sola fide* who is able to speak meaningfully of the relation between the works of faith and reward; he is guarded against the deceit of the human heart which threatens ever to substitute for this relation, grounded in God's mercy, a correlation arranged outside the divine mercy, and through which the religion of faith in God's sovereign grace is seriously endangered.[48]

* * *

3. *The doctrine of justification in the book of James.*   The epistle of James has served as ammunition for many who

---

46. As Peter writes (I Pet. 1:9), "receiving the end of your faith, even the salvation of your souls," Calvin speaks of "the reward of faith." *Institutes*, III, xviii, 3.

47. *Institutes*, III, xviii, 8.

48. What should we say about whether the word *merit* itself should be used?   According to Althaus the old Lutheran theology did not "pedantically ban" the use of the term. Cf. *Die Christliche Wahrheit*, II, p. 470. He is of the personal opinion that the word should be used only in quotation marks to signify that it is not meant literally, and only as a "bold, extreme word of paradox, to the praise of grace." *Ibid.* It is true that the word *merit* appears here and there in sixteenth century Reformed theology, even in confessions, in the Apology, for example, and in Chemnitz. Cf. Chemnitz, *Examen Concilii Tridentini* ed. Preuss, 1861, p. 212. The intent of the word is clear in both the Apology and Chemnitz, and it is obviously not in conflict with *sola fide*. Nevertheless, it is dubious whether the word has a legitimate corner in Christian thought. First, because of

have sought to demonstrate from Scripture that the Reformed doctrine of *sola fide* is a one-sided, partial view of the whole biblical perspective. This appeal concentrates largely on James 2:24: "Ye see that by works a man is justified, and not only by faith." This, at first glance, hardly presents a problem; the Reformed mind is simply set aside, *sola fide* is clearly refuted.

Luther's famous aspersion on the book of James sharpens the polemic, since the reformer's slighting remarks are alleged to indicate that the Reformation, its confessions of the full authority of Scripture notwithstanding, fell into an exegetical and dogmatic subjectivism. Did Luther not write that this epistle could hardly have come from an apostle "since it teaches, in opposition to St. Paul, justification by works"?[49]

Apart from Luther's peculiar attitude toward this letter,[50] we are put before a question in the relation between Paul and James which clamors for answering. If we are going to maintain *sola fide,* we cannot ignore this problem. Calvin, too,

---

49. Cf. J. C. S. Locher, *De leer van Luther over Gods Woord,* 1903, pp. 198 ff.

50. Luther's position as to James's epistle is fairly complicated. Locher points out that, in spite of his minimizing remarks, Luther was not prepared to reject it. In fact, he had great respect for it, providing it was considered not apostolic and took no position amongst the leading epistles. In spite of his contention that James' letter in comparison to those of Paul was "ein recht stroherner Epistel" (truly an epistle of straw), he quotes James frequently without criticism. Johann Haar mentions that Luther cited James 1:18 very often and says: "Luther had a special love for this verse." Cf. J. Haar, *Initium creaturae Dei,* 1939, pp. 28f. Psychologically, the fact that James was constantly being thrown at Luther during his great debates may have had something to do with his impetuous remark.

---

the suspicions it has aroused against itself through its use by the Roman Catholic Church in its doctrine of grace. But even more because of the tension between the idea of merit (which has its proper function only in the combination of work and payment-according-to-right) and the humility and dependence of faith, as much in respect to reward as to anything else. Reformed and Lutheran theology speaks of the merit of Christ, and for this has been criticized for imbibing an element of scholastic theology. Cf. H. Schmid, *Handbuch der Symbolik,* 1890, p. 182. However, Reformed theology actually speaks of the merit of Christ for the very same reason that it has rejected the merit of the believer.

was forced to come to grips with James, for James's letter was used against him as it was against Luther. Calvin, as we shall see, responded with a positive answer, as Luther did not, suggesting that he saw a harmony in the witness of Paul and James which Luther missed.

We may suggest three possible answers to the problem raised by James's relation to Paul, answers that have been given in the past. (1) James is debating with Paul. (This solution assumes that Paul's letter to the Romans was written before James's epistle.) (2) James is contending, not against Paul, but against an antinomian misconstrual of Paul's doctrine of justification through faith. (3) Paul's and James's letters are concerned with different problems, and are not in the least contending with each other. They are rooted in the same assumptions and are in no way incompatible.

* * *

The last construction mentioned is often criticized as an *a priori* assertion based on a dogmatic doctrine of Scripture. Calvin, we are reminded, said in this connection, "That the Spirit is not inconsistent with Himself, is a certain truth."[51] Certainly such an *a priori* is not gathered from an exegesis of the actual words, and, on the basis of James's letter, hardly supportable.

For impartial readers, we are told, the contradiction is perfectly self-evident. F. C. Baur, for example, says that there is a "real difference, a distinct contradiction" between James and Paul on the doctrine of justification. Consistently, the works which Paul rejects, justify according to James, and faith, which according to James has no significance without works, has justifying power according to Paul.[52] Baur rejects any attempt to force a compromise, such as the idea that

51. *Institutes*, III, xvii, 11.
52. F. Chr. Baur, *Paulus, der Apostel Jesu Christi*. 2nd. ed., 1867, II, pp. 322 ff.

Paul and James mean something different by the word justification, Paul meaning the real thing and James its manifestation.   What Baur calls a forced compromise, however, is put forward by many who do not read in James anything contrary to Paul.   This was, indeed, Calvin's answer to those who paraded James's words as the Achilles' heel of the Reformation.   According to Calvin, Paul wished to show how it is that God accounts us as righteous, while James is concerned with the proofs of justification in its fruits.[53]

We could approach this problem through the chronological relation between Paul and James.   Can it be maintained that Paul's Roman epistle precedes James?   If it cannot, the idea of the polemics dissolves.   But a material agreement between the two would hardly thereby be substantiated.   It would mean, however, that Paul and James could have been writing in different phases of development and could therefore have had different problems before them.   Still, the central problem does not lie here.   Besides, in a discussion such as this, we should limit ourselves as much as possible to the words of Scripture.[54]

Apart from everything else, it is certainly clear that James is concerned with those who have not understood nor brought into practice the close connection between faith and works. He preaches this connection anew, as appears from his words: "What doth it profit, my brethren, if a man say he hath faith, but have not works?   Can that faith save him?" (James 2:14).   This questioning of the worth and the power of faith suggests a threat to the Christian life among his readers, a total misunderstanding, an abstract concept of faith that is sealed off from the whole network of its experienced realities.

---

53. Calvin, *Commentary on James*, cf. commentary on James 2:21 ff.
54. The arguments for an early dating of James are internal: the idea of the Diaspora; the aiming of the letter at Jewish Christians, which, it is said, could indicate that the great conversion of Gentiles to the Church had not yet occured; and, finally, the fact that many terms used by James still have a strongly implicit character.

James evidently has a definite situation in mind, a situation in which faith is taken to be the human function of taking a certain position and accepting, or believing, given truths.

It is important to keep James's design before us. For, at least on this point, there is no divergence from Paul. We have already noted Paul's feeling about such a notion of faith when we discussed the importance to him of the judgment according to works. James specifies a necessary marriage of works to faith and in that concurs with Paul's insistence on the fruits of the Spirit (Gal. 5:22), on faith working through love (Gal. 5:6), on the work of faith (I Thess. 2:13), and on the impossibility that those who have died to sin could live in it any longer (Rom. 6:2). James, too, opposes real to dead faith: "if a man *says* he has faith." He offers no academic treatise on faith, no definition; he sets his feet in living reality. Is there a man who contends that he has faith, but has no works? His faith will not save him. Such a faith bodes no reason for confidence as it faces the eschatological judgment. This is the earnestness of James's question, for to him, as appears in other portions of his letter (James 5:7-9), all of life is bathed in this eschatological light. The neighbor — hungry and ragged — comes in sight here, even as he does in Jesus's eschatological discourse (Matt. 25). What has *this* faith to do with a down-and-out neighbor? Fine talk and no act of help leaves him where he was. Such is faith when it is not incarnate in works: barren, dry, dead. Itself dead, it cannot reach out to life.

Up to this point, James's meaning is certainly clear.

Now, before he brings in Abraham to strengthen his argument, he adds another statement that has long proved a riddle. "Yea, a man will say, Thou hast faith, and I have works: show me thy faith apart from thy works, and I by my works will show thee my faith" (James 2:18). Without going into the matter too extensively we should say that the verse contends against the divorce of faith and works. James puts that contention into the mouth of another: Show me your faith, your fruitless faith, your faith without works; so far as I can see, it remains a mere assertion.

James infers that there is good reason to sit down and give this phenomenon of faith a critical survey. A phenomeno-logical analysis of believing will not do. For, you believe, do you not, that there is but one God? Good, but even the devils believe that, and tremble (James 2:19). This is suggestive, this comparison with demonic faith: empty faith can be exposed by a remark about demons, who are hardly atheists, who believe and quake. It must by now be understood what dubious worth this mere faith has. But this "merely believe" is quite another thing than Paul's "through faith alone." For the mere faith that James is against is existentially aloof from its object. The depth of the necessary personal relation is lacking. Such a "believer" may yield to apologetic argu-ment, he may even be over-powered by the force of revelation, but he stands where he was before, and there he trembles.

* * *

The argument that James contradicts Paul draws its most impressive support from James's reference to the patriarch Abraham. Paul had used the figure of Abraham to say that a man is justified without works, through faith alone. James uses him to show that "mere faith" is insufficient. The thought streams of the two apostles cross each other, with Abraham, the father of believers, the point of intersection. If it had been two other apostles it would not be particularly worthy of note. But James and Paul! How is it possible that Paul sees in our father Abraham the peculiar significance of faith without works (Rom. 4), while James, having set Abraham on the stage, says, "Do you not now see that man is justified through works and not only by faith?" (James 2:24). Abraham seems to have been caught up in the eddy of interpre-tation and become all things to all men. In all intellectual honesty, can we still confess the harmony of the Scriptures here?

There is little or no disagreement as to James's intent. Roman Catholic and Protestant alike realize James is saying that faith without works is fruitless and dead. But the Catholic will go on to say that James's words are an authoritative elucidation of Paul's letters to the Romans and Galatians. James, then, gets the primacy, at least as to clarity. With the problem so posed — James as Paul's interpreter — we have special reason to consider with care the message which James, under the guidance of the Holy Spirit, has brought.

To begin with, James does not make his reference to Abraham from the same portion of Genesis as did Paul. Paul, recall, cited Genesis 15:6: "Abraham believed God, and it was reckoned to him for righteousness" (Rom. 4:3). James starts from Genesis 22, the reference being to Abraham's willingness to offer his son Isaac. "Was not Abraham our father justified by works, in that he offered up Isaac his son upon the altar?" (James 2:21). This difference in reference is essential to an understanding of James, as we shall attempt to show. What the angel said to Abraham is also important: "By myself have I sworn, saith Jehovah, because thou hast not withheld thy son, thine only son, that in blessing I will bless thee, and in multiplying I will multiply thy seed as the stars of the heavens, and as the sand which is upon the seashore; and thy seed shall possess the gate of his enemies; and in thy seed shall all the nations of the earth be blessed; because thou hast obeyed my voice" (Gen. 22:15-18).

As to this "work," this act of faith, James makes the surprising statement that the Scripture is therewith fulfilled, which says: "And Abraham believed God and it was reckoned unto him for righteousness; and he was called the friend of God" (James 2:23). James too, then, quotes the text from Genesis 15 which Paul had used. But James cites it in a special connection; Genesis 15 is *fulfilled* in what occurs in

Genesis 22.   Faith and work — James sees their inter-woven congruency over the totality of life.   The whole life of Abraham was *lived* in faith.

This faith was not something isolated, an abstract acceptance of something as true, but a truly experienced reality that dominated this entire existence.   This faith, since it can be understood only in its movement toward its object, gives God the honor in its limitless confidence in Him, and therefore is expressed in obedience.   The statement of Genesis 15:6 is seen as fulfilled, completed, incarnated in the concrete reality of Abraham's obedience of Genesis 22.   This appears as well when James writes that Abraham's faith is perfected in his works.   James obviously does not mean to say that Abraham's faith was at first imperfect, incomplete, and then, gradually, was perfected in concrete existence.   In the command given to Abraham lies the touchstone of his faith, and in his obedience Abraham's faith was revealed as real in the reality of life.   "If when the test came, the faith had not been matched by works, then it would have been proved to be an incomplete faith.   The works showed that the faith had always been of the right kind and so 'completed it.' "[55]   This is what James wants to say in his entire discourse on the relation between faith and works.   And if he is thus understood it is hard to see how anyone can seriously put a cleavage between him and Paul.

That they are agreed is more than established when James says that Abraham's faith expressed itself in cooperation with his works.   This is to say that Abraham's concrete life manifested such a cohesion of faith and works that they could not be pulled apart.   He who still insists that James wishes to establish works as another element independent of and alongside of faith simply has not grasped the sense of his exhortation.

55. J. H. Ropes, *The Epistle of St. James*, in the *International Critical Commentary*, 1916, p. 220.

It is striking that James does not say that works cooperate with faith, but faith with works. Here we encounter the principial homogeneity of faith and works. To insist that faith and works are "made for each other" need not suggest an argument with the Pauline phrase "justified by faith alone." James does not devaluate faith. We put a touchstone only to that which we value highly; and this is what James does, too. He does not deny that faith saves, claiming that it is not sufficient and must be complemented by works. The faith which he contests is *dead* faith, and of such he asks, Can *that* faith save him?

In short, James's point is this — true faith is not dead, empty, or fruitless. It is experienced in the daily reality of human life. Be James's letter directed against whom it may, it is not aimed at Paul. For if Paul sets faith and righteousness of faith against works (Rom. 3:28) it is against the works of the law, not works done in and out of faith. And James adds to this that there is no split between true faith and good works. "There is absolutely no possible thought that James's polemic strikes against Paul." Any one who knows Paul, says Kittel further, must recognize "that whatever James polemicizes against, it is certainly not the theology of Paul, but something which, though similar perhaps, is yet absolutely different from it."[56]

That this whole James vs. Paul affair could have arisen at all is only ascribable to a failure to distinguish between works of the law and the works of faith. If we faithfully make this distinction, we shall also be able to understand the final line that James adds to his study of Abraham: "Ye see that by works a man is justified, and not only by faith" (James 2:24). This last phrase — not only by faith — could turn a man from the "one-sided" Paulinism of the reformers, if he were satisfied with a superficial reading. But understand it in the context of James's whole work, and it takes on the true accents of the

---

56. Kittel, *Theologisches Wörterbuch zum N. T.*, IV. p. 95.

gospel as preached by Paul and all the apostles, for it is directed against the fruitless, dead faith which is not real faith at all, which is the same as the faith of the demons who believe and only tremble. James keeps hammering on this anvil. In the example of Rahab, too, he repeats that faith without works is not faith. And, again, at the close of his discussion, he says, "For as the body apart from the spirit is dead, even so faith apart from works is dead" (James 2:26).

James's warning is of elemental, evangelical significance. It seeks to set us more firmly and really upon the foundation laid in Jesus Christ. It is a pity that Luther, led as he was by reaction, was unable to see that James's epistle was deeply harmonious with the message of the gospel — and with every struggle motivated by the gospel against antinomianism and any doctrine of faith that at bottom escaped the reality of life. James is a particularly fine example of the profound concord within the one Word, the Word that introduces our life into the circle of the reality of God's grace and thereby into the seriousness of faith.

The voice of James sounding through the congregation does not call us back from a wholehearted trust in divine grace, the grace that saves apart from the works of the law. It calls us up to a real, existential trust which, fastened on grace, stands in the freedom of Christ. Hence, life in faith becomes life in the world where faith is revealed in works, and is thereby revealed as true faith.

Both lines meet in Abraham. Paul can appeal to Abraham in order to avoid any form of religious self-confidence which refuses to honor grace as radical, sovereign, divine. James can find in Abraham the *nature* of faith in its true expression. And yet so many debates have waged around James and Paul. We have, perhaps, made too static the dogmatic content of certain New Testament terms. We must ever search the apostolic letters for the profound religious train of thought that defines the argument of each book. That faithfully done, we shall find reason to rejoice over the varied, and yet not contradicting, aspects of the New Testament. In this case, we find the one central message in two deeply unified strains: on one side we are warned against religious self-confidence, on the other against a faith which is not really directed to God's grace in Jesus Christ, and is and remains dead.

James, finally, points to the coming of the husbandman "who waiteth for the precious fruit of the land" (James 5:7). He preaches the coming of the judgment to the dispersed congregation, reminding them, and us, that the judgment according to works searches out the reality of faith, not alongside of, but *in* our daily lives. James wants to clear the doctrine of faith of any illusiveness. He wants to say that faith does not create an ideal world of fancy for us. Faith, true faith, carries us into the world of this day and the next. There and there only shall faith save through its grasp on grace which impels us toward a life really lived in profound thankfulness.

*   *   *

We have in this chapter discussed various objections that have been raised repeatedly against justification by faith alone. It has, I trust, become somewhat clearer that the final judgment according to works, the promise of rewards, and the message of James are all bound together by one central issue. These portions of Scripture must never be driven into the background. To allow that is not only to impoverish the inheritance of the Reformation, but to dim the lights of Scripture and of grace. For faith has everything to do with living in both the breath-taking whirl and the tedious tread-mill of life. Faith is directed to God's mercy, and just for that reason it is *real* faith, and makes us real people freed from the illusions and delusions of sinful living. The preaching of the gospel must always speak to real life, warning against the abstractness and self-complacency of the doctrine of "merely believe."

But this preaching does not compete with the *sola fide* of the Reformation. Wholly otherwise! Only through *sola fide* does it get its real force. Where *sola fide* is one with *sola gratia,* grace becomes our atmosphere and our foothold. We are led by faith into the reality of the secret which bound Paul and James together as men of one idea and one simple faith: "And if Christ is in you, the body is dead because of sin; but the spirit is life because of righteousness" (Rom. 8:10).

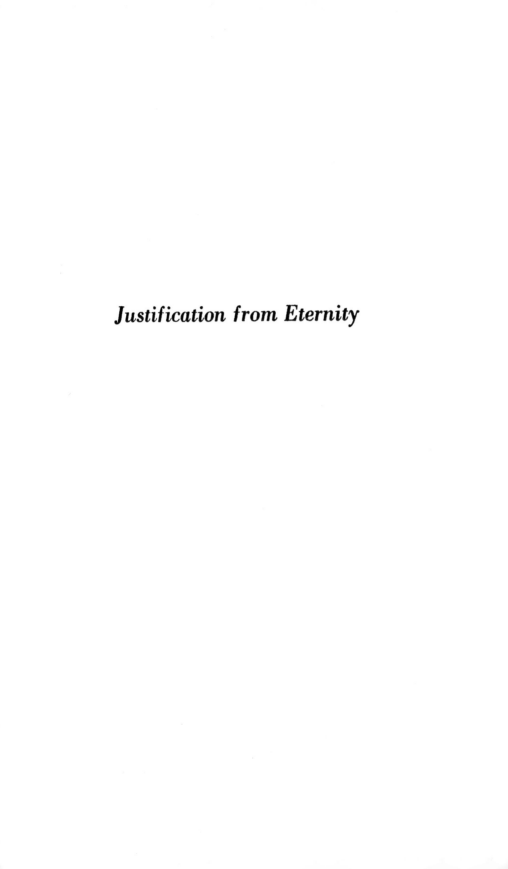

Justification from Eternity

CHAPTER VI

Justification from Eternity

ARE we now to entangle ourselves in a subtle, scholastic puzzle about justification from eternity, an academic problem which promises only to remove us from the living reality of simple faith? We must admit that theologians have at times played with this question as though it were an innocent speculation, and have done so to the pain and sorrow of the Church. But even as they puzzled, those who were earnest enough saw that there was an issue involved which did touch a vital area of Christian faith. At the present time, it is recognized that this old problem has facets which are acutely relevant. It was Verschoor who said of a debate over this problem between Comrie and Brakel "that Comrie's *No* to Brakel was as violent as Barth's *No* to Brunner, and that, in the deepest sense, both had to do with the same issue."

The debate about justification from eternity is conditioned by the nature of the relation between faith and justification. The question was whether justification occurs completely *in time,* thus making sense of the phrase "justification through faith," or whether it precedes faith as such and occurs in the eternity of God's counsel. If the latter were true, it would still be possible to speak of a justification through faith in time, but the justification in time would be viewed only against the more profound and decisive background of justification in eternity. The issue, and it is necessary to keep this in mind, is not correctly proposed in the antithesis *justification in time vs. justification from eternity.* Those who have taught justification from eternity have almost always insisted that this did not exclude a justification through faith in time. To explain this they sometimes suggested various "stages" in justification.

Kuyper, an exponent of justification from eternity, saw five steps in justification: the counsel of God, the resurrection of Christ, the planting of capacity for faith in man, the daily exercise of faith, and the last judgment.[1] Thus, though he taught justification from eternity, he did not, as the steps show, rule out a justification in time. It is not, then, a question of two mutually exclusive doctrines. The deepest issue of this debate had to do not with logic, but with the relation of the sinner to God.

Kuyper emphasized that justification was a matter of our *status* before God, of His gracious imputation of Christ's righteousness, of the putting forward of Christ Himself. He confessed, naturally, that the sinner is justified through faith, but felt too that all would be lost if faith were looked on as an act of human merit which exercises a constitutive and determinative function for justification. Here we touch again the problem that has occupied our attention continually in this study — the place, significance, and function of faith in justification. For Kuyper this was at issue in the problem of justification from eternity. He wanted to say that, in the correlation of faith and justification, the latter does not originate through faith, but that is only *accepted* in and through faith.[2] This is the standpoint from which Kuyper argues for justification from eternity.

---

1. A. Kuyper, *E Voto*, II, p. 333. In his *Loci* (*De Salute*, IV) Kuyper has nine steps: the decree, *Constitutio Mediatoris*, presentation of Christ's sacrifice, resurrection of Christ, planting of capacity for faith, preaching of the gospel, the actual believing, continuous conversion, and the last judgment.

2. This comes out clearly when Kuyper writes: "This is now justification through faith. Not that which comes into being through faith. Not that which first begins to work through faith. Not even that which, as though it were still defective, is completed through faith. No! Your justification lay complete and perfect outside of you when you approached it through faith. All that your faith does is believe it, and in faith accept it." *E Voto*, II, p. 344.

If justification is a divine act of grace which no human merit can achieve, then it must also precede faith, argues Kuyper, as eternity "precedes" time. In developing this idea Kuyper adds that justification need not wait upon the revelation in time of conversion, consciousness of faith, and so forth. The sovereign act of justification arises from the depths of God's secret life as a truly eternal *pre*.[3] Certainly the divine justification is declared and proclaimed at a given moment in time, but this proclamation must be distinguished from justification itself.[4] Justification must be freed from every tie with anything present in us. It is an act of divine sovereignty. Faith is shed of any creative function and retains only what we may call its receptive function.

It is not hard to recognize the profound religious motivation of the Reformation in all this. Without judging at the moment the discreteness of the term *justification from eternity*, we must admit that Kuyper uses it to translate the elementary experience of faith of every simple believer. For at heart every believer knows that his faith witnesses to and honors the sovereignly free grace of a divine act.

From this sovereign freedom, this independence, of God's act, Kuyper concludes that the essential, the eternal justification comes to life in our consciousness in the justification which is through faith. The assumption is that justification has already been prepared for us before it enters our consciousness. By faith justification is appropriated in our consciousness and accepted in its eternal validity.[5]

---

3. Cf. A. Kuyper, *Het Werk van de Heilige Geest,* 2nd ed., 1927, p. 462: "Whenever a child of God reflects with his soul on the glorious and delightful reality of his justification, he does not feel confined to the moment of his conversion or to any other moment of the past; he feels how his salvation flowed out to him from eternal depths of the secret life of his God."

4. *Ibid.,* p. 463; cf. *E Voto,* II, p. 335.

5. Cf. Kuyper, *Loci* IV. p. 64: "Bread does not become bread through the eating of it; it must be bread in order to be eaten. Eating only involves the perception and appropriation of it."

Kuyper's views did not go without opposition. How, it was asked, if justification is an eternal fact, is it possible to speak seriously of a justification through faith in time? All that remains is for the believer *to become conscious of his justification*. It was said, further, that what is present in God's eternal knowledge, does not as such exist in historical reality. Galatians 3:8 was quoted against Kuyper. "And the Scripture, foreseeing that God would justify the Gentiles by faith, preached the gospel beforehand unto Abraham, saying, In thee shall all the nations be blessed." The Gentiles, then, were not yet justified; they were yet to be made righteous. That is to say, justification was yet to take place *in time through faith*. Justification as an act of God has always been exhibited among His *historical works*. Eternal justification, therefore, cannot be a dogma of the Church. So went the argument against Kuyper.

Bavinck refuted the idea of eternal justification by getting at its underlying religious motive. He began by pointing out that Reformed theology has ever taken great care to avoid antinomianism and, in doing so, has also rejected unequivocally the doctrine of eternal justification. He was careful, however, to distinguish antinomianism from English antineonomianism. This latter antineonomianism protested against an interpretation of the gospel which read faith as a cooperating cause of our justification. The antineonomians insisted on the instrumental character of faith according to which faith was concerned exclusively with the content of its object. Justification from eternity was sometimes affirmed, but then not as the be all and end all of salvation. The great significance of justification through faith in time was fully appreciated; and this was in contrast to antinomianism which had no place at all for justification in time, construing it only as a declaration of the justification which existed eternally.

Bavinck acknowledged the religious motivation of the antineonomians. They were concerned with the pure gospel of grace and "kept alive a precious truth in eternal justification, a truth which no Reformed thinker may nor shall deny."[6] Bavinck also confessed that neither time nor anything occurring in time is detached from eternity: "Justification could never take its place in time were it not established in eternity."[7] He perceived the dimension of depth in the justifying act of God and saw, too, that it was this from which men like Kuyper drew the doctrine of eternal justification.

And yet Bavinck disputes the legitimacy of an eternal justification, or justification from eternity. He does so, first, because the Scriptures nowhere speak of it. Furthermore, he said, if one speaks of justification as eternal he should consistently also speak of creation, incarnation, sacrifice, calling, and regeneration as eternal. He was grateful that Reformation theology generally, from fear of antinomianism, had shied away from the idea.[8] He was happy, too, he said, that even those who, under the mantle of Reformed theology, accepted the doctrine of eternal justification never maintained that the covenant of peace (the *pactum salutis*) was justification, entire and complete.

Thus, though Bavinck rejected the doctrine of justification from eternity, he still moved materially within the line of Kuyper, at least in his religious intention to hold untainted the confession of grace. He thought it most important that "Reformed theology hold fast to the truth that all the benefits of the covenant of grace are established in eternity."[9] Bavinck's careful distinctions are of weight in this discussion, since the distinction between antinomian speculation and antineonomianism must be kept in mind if the whole discussion is to be understood.

Others thought they perceived a sharper distinction between eternal justification and justification in time than that ad-

---

6. H. Bavinck, *Gereformeerde Dogmatiek*, IV. p. 199.
7. *Ibid.*
8. *Ibid.*, III, p. 589.
9. *Ibid.*, p. 599.

mitted by Bavinck. According to this group, justification from
eternity allows for only an acknowledgement of justification
in time. If this is so, then there is no *real* justification in time.
They saw a speculative element in the doctrine which minimized what took place in time and threw everything important
back into eternity. It was the Reformed counterpart of idealism. It was part of the picture, then, that the same opponents
of eternal justification should oppose supralapsarianism[10] and
the so-called eternal covenant of grace, as well as the identi-
fication of the covenant of peace with the covenant of grace.
The Scriptures, they contended, present justification ever in
connection with faith. They wanted to underline, to put in
italics, that the *significance of faith is real* and justification by
faith not a mere eye-opener to the fact that one has already
been justified.

This brings in our old friend, the problem of the relation
between time and eternity. Both parties in the discussion on
eternal justification are perpetually speaking of what happens
in time and what in eternity. One somehow senses that in
each solution there is something vaguely unsatisfactory, and
that this has something to do with the profound relation of
time to eternity. We note this even more in the still earlier
debates on our present question.

The earlier discussions were consistently connected in one
way or another with antinomianism. This antinomianism is
not simply a radical disavowal of the validity of the law in the
life of believers. The antinomianism we are dealing with here
has far reaching implications for the work of Christ and for
the doctrine of justification. Antinomianism tirelessly preached
the completely and perfectly finished work of Christ on the
cross. Redemption was accomplished in this unrepeatable and
definitive event, and from this it was concluded that there is

---

10. Cf. W. Heyns, *Manual of Reformed Doctrine*, 1926, p. 239: "Thus
supra presents justification as having been accomplished in eternity and
thus a benefit for which faith can have no signification. The necessity of
faith for justification as a judicial act of God is eliminated."

really nothing for the believer to do, that every effort to ascribe
an activity to the believer was a refined form of work-righteousness, and that this was an attempt to add self-righteousness to the work of Christ as though His work were insufficient. At first sight, all this may sound like a revival of
Pauline preaching — the total decisiveness and exclusive significance of the righteousness of Christ.

Bavinck realized that antinomianism contained an element
of truth which we shall have to digest if we are to set up
resistance to antinomianism as such.[11] The error of the antinomians was not that they hearkened back to Christ's perfect
work. The Reformers, too, were forced to recall the "once for
all-ness" of Christ's sacrifice when faced with the Roman mass
and its repetition of Christ's death. How often in their controversy did they not pen the words of Christ's high-priestly
prayer: "I glorified thee on earth, having accomplished the
work which thou hast given me to do" (John 17:4)? The
extent of Christ's sacrifice is universal, absorbing the shocks
of sin and death, rolling over ages, sifting the sands of time,
penetrating the hard shell of man's secret individuality. How
can man add anything to this, which is celebrated in heaven
perpetually with the ultimate paean of praise: "Worthy art
thou . . . for thou wast slain, and didst purchase unto God with
thy blood men of every tribe, and tongue, and people, and
nation . . ." (Rev. 5:9)?

Had antinomianism done nothing else than remind the
world of this perfect offering for the sins of the world, it
would have been embraced into the fold of the Reformation
sola fide. But the fact is that the antinomians drew a great
deal of bitter water from the well of their primal conviction.
They concluded that all sin and guilt, all taint and impurity
were swept away and were now not merely disallowed, but
impossible. Sin as guilt before God could no longer exist in
the believer.

---

11. Bavinck, *Gereformeerde Dogmatiek*, III, p. 571.

Forgiveness was so immense that at the moment in which actual sin threatened to invade the life of the believer, it was sucked away into the, vacuum of eternal redemption. Prayer for forgiveness, as the Lord had taught it, was not for believers. Redemption was locked up so tight in eternity that what happened in time could no longer touch it. Such a turn of logic could not find its home in anything temporal. The thinking of antinomianism came to rest finally in the doctrine of eternal justification. The decision was made in God's decree; justification was set in eternal granite. Our sins were annuled in eternal simultaneity with the divine decree of justification.

This concept of eternal justification reveals how a speculative logic can invade a scriptural proclamation of salvation and torture it beyond recognition. This is the danger of an apparently consistent logical process which at first imperceptibly and then quite finally estranges itself from scriptural reality. The fault of the thinking is not that it refuses to let the divine acting and speaking in time loose from the grip of eternity nor that it refuses to lose the redeeming work of Christ in the maze of historical relativity. It lies in this, that it robs the divine revelation of its unique and saving significance and devaluates the historical character of the activity of God. When speculation on time and eternity, with eternity swallowing up the significance of time, determines the line of thought, there is no possibility of doing justice to such mysteries as the incarnation and redemption — or to justification through faith within the temporal reality of our lives.

Having reached this extreme, opposition to nomism could bear no fruit. Had antinomianism merely disavowed that faith was a condition precedent to justification, it could still have maintained the real character of the correlation between faith and justification, and with this could have withstood the nomism which makes a *causal* relation out of this correlation. But it reacted too severely and lost its grasp on the fact that God pronounces His judgment of justification in the way of faith through the preaching of redemption within our temporal existence. The reality of justification in time must never be by-passed via a speculative train of thought concerning eternity. He who allows justification and redemption to ascend out of time into eternity is never again able to avoid the fatal conclusion that everything occurring in time merely formalizes or illustrates what has been molded in eternal quietness. Even the terrible reality of the cross is swallowed in the deep, still waters of eternity.

Between this antinomianism and the idealism of the nineteenth century there is a remarkable correspondence. The analogy lies in antinomianism's concept of time and eternity and idealism's construal of idea and fact. Both debase time and history, as well as God's decisive invasion of history. These people are groping beyond history and behind time for the real revelation. Both view the revelation of God, not as real revelation, but as an illustration of the true, eternal idea. To take this line of approach in Christian thought is to fall into a morass of speculation. Antinomianism is a sorry chapter in the Church's history, but it can serve well as a sharp warning to every member of the Church that the way of Christian truth is not the thin thread of speculation, but the concrete revelation of God in Word and Act.

* * *

With an eye to the example of antinomianism, later protagonists of the doctrine of eternal justification were careful to allow for the vital significance of justification through faith in time. Kuyper, whom we have previously mentioned as a teacher of justification from eternity, spoke of justification through faith as the "artery of grace." Nevertheless, we can detect a certain tension present in the whole discussion of justification from eternity. On one hand, there were men who

were eager not to over-estimate the importance of faith in
justification and who therefore gave unreserved priority to
the justifying act of God over the faith which received and
accepted this judgment. The next step from this was the
doctrine of eternal justification. On the other hand, other
thinkers, eager to preserve the significance of faith, accented,
with Scripture presumably, the call to believe and taught that
justification follows upon faith. Hereby the danger of neonomianism showed its ugly head. We see in antinomianism
and neonomianism the two principle possibilities by which the
correlation between faith and justification may be miscon-
strued.

A debate which took place in the Netherlands of the eighteenth century between Brakel and Comrie illustrates the fact
that we have here touched upon the heart of the question concerning the correlation between faith and justification. Brakel
wanted a sharp distinction between the purpose of God and
justification itself. God, he said, decreed from eternity to
justify, but this decree is not justification as such.[12] The elect,
according to Ephesians 2:3 and Romans 5:10, are, before they
are regenerated, children of wrath by nature and enemies of
God. This could not be asserted in Scripture if they really had
been justified from eternity. Justification occurs, according
to Brakel, after the sinner is called and through the means of
actual faith, thus it cannot be from eternity. This was self-
evident to Brakel: faith must precede justification. Only after
faith takes hold of Christ and His benefits does God come with
His justifying declaration of pardon. We could perhaps call
this an analytical justification, meaning that the believer clothes
himself through faith with Christ's righteousness and as so
garbed is declared justified. This is not, says Brakel, to be
confused with justification through works; justification occurs
only through faith, which is to say, through the righteousness

12. For Brakel's side of the discussion, vid. W. à Brakel, *Redelijke
Godsdienst,* 2nd ed., 1893, I, pp. 855 ff.

of Christ as it is assumed through faith. Faith is not presented as the cause of the believer's righteousness, but as a means of accepting Christ's righteousness; the notion that love and obedience to the commands of Christ justify is rejected. Faith, then, is not a work, but a means. Otherwise justification would be, after all, through works. Brakel avers that his conception is scriptural, that he insists with the Bible that man is not justified *because* of faith, that faith is not a meritorious cause, ground, or rationale of justification. Justification, he says, is only *through* Christ as received in faith.

Brakel's intent is clearly to identify his thought, with the Reformation *sola fide*. Faith is presented as directed toward its object and content, and only in this connection does it have significance. Not the work of faith, nor the psychological attitude involved in believing, but the direction and content is the thing.

But at this point Brakel begins to sing in his own theological key. Justification is possessed by the believer as the result of his having taken upon himself through faith the righteousness of Christ. Divine justification is more like an infallible observation of the actual state of affairs, of the righteousness which is present in the believer, than a sovereign, justifying declaration. Though it be true that Brakel lets the weight of his argument fall on the righteousness of Christ as the meriting cause of justification, he must admit that justification, in his view, is an analytical process, not a synthetic judgment. Brakel must have known that, according to Paul, it is the *ungodly* whom God declares righteous.

We may now introduce Alexander Comrie, Brakel's contemporary and greatest opponent, into the discussion.[13] Comrie suspected Brakel's teaching of being tainted with Arminianism. It was Brakel's insistence that faith comes before

---

13. Comri's thought may best be gathered from his *Brief over de recht-vaardiging des zondaars door de onmiddelijk toerekening der borggerech-tigheid van Christus*, 1889 ed.

the assumption of the righteousness of Christ which led to
Comrie's charge. The soul of the remonstrants' appeal was
that man is justified through the *act* of faith. For Comrie it
was the sovereign grace of God, the grace that preceded faith
which was written in boldface and to which faith is merely an
answer. Faith is not the work, but the instrument. It was a
short step, then, to the position that justification takes temporal
precedence to faith or, better, that justification is eternal,
before all time, while faith is a mere temporal assent to an
eternal truth. The relation of faith and justification was
neither reciprocal, nor causal; the very existence of the relation was brought into being by God's previous gracious act of
justification. At the heart of Comrie's appeal was a fervent
desire that grace be not dependent upon the subjectivity of
man's faith.

It was certainly not Brakel's intent to make a meritorious
human function out of faith. And yet, admitting his sincere
confession of justification by grace, we must still say that his
thesis that faith preceded justification made him blind in one
eye to the Reformation doctrine of justification. Comrie, on
the other hand, apart from the peculiar form of his argument,
really did move back toward the Reformation theme. But did
he avoid the Charybdis Arminianism only to go aground on
the Scylla antinomianism?

He did not want to deny justification through faith, any
more than Kuyper did. Thus he had to think hard about the
relation between justification in time and justification from
eternity. His conclusion was that justification goes back to
eternity. He defended the justification of the ungodly against
what he called the "new doctrine" of the priority of faith to
justification. We may rightly speak, says, Comrie, of a justification through faith, but only with the understanding that
there is first a justification before faith and unto faith. This
must be so since justification is first of all an act of God quite
external to us. Accordingly, he rejected the thesis that faith

is a precondition which must be fulfilled before God imputes the righteousness of Christ to us. In other words, he opposed those who averred divine justification to be not previous to, but only of and through and, indeed, because of and after our believing. Comrie did not devaluate what occurs or shall, according to God's will, occur in time and was amazed that he should be charged with denying the importance of "justification through faith." He was not willing, however, to let a jot or tittle be removed from the truth that God's love and grace do not arise from time or from the relativity of human experience. Grace is from eternity and is the real source of everything that God stoops to give us in time. Thus, it must simply be a fact that justification is eternal, founded in the eternal God. To deny this is to invite the specter of Arminianism and neonomianism, for to deny it is to say that justification waits on human acts of faith. As Brakel taught an analytical justification, so Comrie presents us with a synthetic justification.

There is nothing in man, from the puniest achievement to the noblest accomplishment, which could be the basis for God's justification of him. It is the ungodly whom God justifies. To say anything else is to slide back into Roman Catholic theology, which makes sanctification prior to justification. From all this, it is clear how intense Comrie's desire was to preserve the gracious character of justification in the Reformation sense. It would be ingrate not to appreciate Comrie's defense of the sovereign character of grace or his opposition to an inflated valuation of human works or even of faith. We should credit him with seeing not only that the imagined merit of good works threatens the prize of grace, but that even a pious overvaluation of faith can be an irreligious trespass on work-righteousness. This is quite another thing than the airy speculations of the antinomians, who used the same terms, but filled them with different stuff. Antinomianism scorned time and history, disdained the concrete reality of the temporal, and went in search only of eternal truths. Comrie did not turn to eternity because he found that time had so little to offer. What he wanted to say was that man's precious salvation is established in the depth and riches of the justifying grace of God. And he did not want the priority of this divine grace to go begging for recognition.

* * *

What must we say of all this? It would certainly be untrue, though understandable, to say that it all amounts only to a speculative aberration in the history of theology. Especially in the nineteenth century, when the historical character of divine revelation was forgotten in a flourish of theological and philosophical "eternal concepts," a person trying to hold on to the real and actual events of scriptural revelation might have been inclined to shudder at the word *eternity* in connection with so vital a thing as justification. There have been a good many speculations on eternity whose "ideal world" snuffed out the lights of this temporal existence, though they were acknowledged to have been lighted by God Himself. It is indeed good to beware of such *Zeitlosigkeits-metaphysik*. It plants the kiss of death on eschatology, and on the *way of salvation* and the doctrine of justification as well.

On the other hand, we must say, a reaction to such timeless metaphysics must not drive us to historicize God's work. We see again and again that Scripture accents the realness of revelation in time, but yet impresses us in each reading that His is the revelation of the eternal God. Only unfounded reaction can close our eyes to the dimension of depth in the divine revelation and in His act of redemption. It is this dimension that inspires the canticles and psalms to eternal grace. "Even as he chose us in him before the foundation of the world, that we should be holy and without blemish before him in love: having foreordained us unto adoption as sons through Jesus Christ unto himself, according to the good pleasure of his will, to the praise of the glory of his grace which he freely bestowed on us in the Beloved" (Eph. 1:4-6).

And this is not an isolated aria, nor the only time that the everlasting "before" is sung. God's saving secret hidden from the wise and well-born, is revealed to children: "yea, Father, for so it was well-pleasing in thy sight" (Matt. 11:26). The mystery of His will is made known, according to the pleasure "which He purposed in Him" (Eph. 1:9). In Christ we receive the inheritance, it "having been foreordained according to the purpose of him who worketh all things after the counsel of his will" (Eph. 1:11). His will is conditioned neither by history or the works of individual men (Rom. 9:11). Thus speak the Scriptures of the elective purpose of God.

We shall not discuss the scriptural design of election; it is enough to note here that this Bible message is so plain and assertive that to anyone who takes pains to listen the priority of God's grace will be overwhelmingly convincing. For this reason it is rather remarkable that not election but justification is at issue in most discussions about justification from eternity. This suggests that there is a common antipathy to the humanization of divine grace, and opens the possibility that perhaps the whole debate was clouded by a failure of both sides to understand each other's terms. Everyone in this discussion was committed to both the sovereign character of grace and the necessity of faith.   The differences were in emphasis; different phrases were underlined and voices were raised at different points. There were after all two threats to the gospel: Arminianism (and neonomianism) and antinomianism. One party in our discussion had his eye to the former, the other was dead afraid of the latter. All this was conditioned by differences in personal experiences and temperament, as well as by general outlook on other concerns of the day.

Thus we observe that those who contend for eternal justification are particularly outspoken on behalf of the sovereignty of grace. The opponents of eternal justification, no matter how earnest their confession of eternal election and withal the priority of grace, put the emphasis on the demand of faith, and are most articulate in their serious reminder of the urgent "call to believe." Is there a confessional opposition here? Certainly not at this point. Anyone who reads the confessions seriously knows that they insist upon the necessity of faith as well as that faith in itself carries no merit. The whole gospel can be translated only where both of these facets are included and where both of the dangers they point to are excluded.

It is highly regretable therefore whenever divergences lead to strife instead of to a mutual appreciation of the deepest motives of each. This controversy should now be dead, buried with honors and a tinge of relief. And although the declaration of concord should not mean the discharge of the guards, all those united in an appreciation of the correlation between faith and justification should be able to find and understand each other. The unrestrained goodness of divine grace and the serious call to true faith are alike strains in the one gospel. They do not drown each other out, and neither need we.

*   *   *

We have yet to judge whether a scientific dogmatic opinion allows for the doctrine of eternal justification. To put it another way, does the doctrine of justification from eternity contain a truth which presents the mystery of the correlation between faith and justification more clearly and in a form more full of comfort and warning than does the doctrine of justification as it is expressed in the confessions? As we have mentioned, the opponents of the idea contended that the confessions know of no such notion and the proponents themselves admit that the phrase is not found in any confession. The question is whether the admittedly valid religious motivation behind the doctrine comes satisfactorily to expression in the confessions.

Our opinion is that it does. The confessions assign no creative function to faith in its correlation to justification. The whole matter is framed in God's eternal grace; justification, we are told, does not rest upon the worthiness of our faith but on the eternal precedence of His goodness. That which is intended by the doctrine of eternal justification, the truly illimitable favor of God, must always be the assumption of the correlation between faith and justification. This correlation, however, is given in the confessions as a correlation in time. The sovereignty of grace is honored only in faith, a faith that gives all honor to God. This is why salvation in the historical correlation of faith and justification is made dependent upon human decision. It is this faith which finds its appropriate expression in Jeremiah's confession: "O Jehovah thou hast persuaded me, and I was persuaded; thou art stronger than I, and hast prevailed" (Jer. 20:7).

It was in the midst of our temporal life that the Father revealed Jesus Christ to us in love and redeeming mercy. *Time* is, in Christ, full of His salvation. Salvation is not *of*, but is surely *in* history. It arises out of the eternal depths of the heart of God. The dayspring from on high has visited us because of the mercy of our God (Luke 1:78), and redemption has begun to touch each day's ordinary reality with the light of redemption and renewal (II Cor. 5:17, 18).

The great Worker of salvation is not imprisoned within the walls of time; but it is within them that His word of justification and pardon is heard. And faith is that hearing (Rom. 10:17). We reconcile ourselves to God, as Scripture beseeches us to do (II Cor. 5:20), but in *this* reconciliation we are stripped bare of merit. Thus we may speak of the *way of salvation* and of justification through faith. God's grace as eternal love, as the eternal "precedent" is confessed in this faith. For He died while we were yet sinners (Rom. 5:10). This is the meaning of Christ's words: "You have not chosen me; I have chosen you" (John 15:16), and of John's: "We love him because he first loved us." (I John 4:19).

*   *   *

Thus the very nature of faith itself involves a recognition and confession of the priority of divine grace. The correlation between faith and justification is unthinkable without this confession. The correlation is in time, it can be nowhere else, but it concurs with the eternal love which is the seed-bed of justification.

There must be no contrast between theological reflection and the personal word of Scripture. Dogmatics can do no more than reflect upon the nature and the implications of this correlation; it can never construct a system for the exclusive enjoyment of professional theologians. Theology is not an excursion into the stratosphere that lies beyond scriptural speech in time; it may not travel beyond the borders of faith's perspective. Beyond the word of Scripture we dare not go, in speech or in theological reflection; for it is in this word that God's love in Jesus Christ is revealed. There is nothing beyond that.

Speculation which seeks after "depth" in place of or beside this "practical" word must be directed back to the simple witness of revelation. For the way of independent speculation leads to a dualism between the practical and the theological, between the simplicity of faith and the systematics of reason — and this destroys the correlation given in the depth of divine revelation.

For this reason there is no place for an eternal justification side by side with a justification in time. Naturally we do not mean to confine God's love within time's horizon. We are moved by the fact that the eternity of divine mercy comes to us in the historical revelation and that this is understood and adored only in faith. We have here drawn nigh to an unfathomable mystery in God's eternal love in Jesus Christ.

Many views of God's eternity have done injustice to His eternal election and thus made human activity really determinative. But this need not lead us in reaction to lose our grasp on the fact that God's eternity is not isolated from us, abstract and transcendent beyond time, but is present and immanent in every moment of time.[14] He makes use of time to reveal His eternal thoughts and virtues. He renders time serviceable and shows Himself thus to be the King of Ages, *Rex seculorum.*"[15]

Eternity and time "are not two lines, of which the shorter runs parallel for a while with the other which extends infinitely; eternity is the unchangeable center which sends out rays to cover the whole contour of time."[16] We all feel the inadequacy of such a formulation, but it helps us understand that we may not search beyond God's historical revelation for a deeper basis and profounder understanding of redemption than that brought into the valley of our temporality by the eternal Son of God Himself. The boundary separating eternal speculations from the reflection of faith lies here: speculation attempts to pierce through into the shades of eternity; faith reflects on the Word given in time and seeks an understanding of the nature of faith itself. This is why true faith when it has arrived at the borders of its terrain, is content to confess God's own eternal election, confessing, then, *sola gratia* and singing the Church's psalm of praise. The conflicts of the Church with Pelagianism, semi-Pelagianism, Arminianism, and all who have denied election were not enflamed by a theological imperialism; they were simply stubborn refusals to be lured by human speculation beyond the confession of sovereign grace as taught in divine revelation.

The Church has exalted divine grace in her confession of justification through faith alone and has said therein just about everything the believer can say of this justification. This con-

---

14. Cf. H. Bavinck, *Gereformeerde Dogmatiek,* II, p. 134.
15. *Ibid.*
16. *Ibid.,* p. 393.

fession needs no amplification; it is complete. Addition to it would be superfluous, for in it the believing soul hears the beating of the Father's heart. Thus we do not need the phrase *eternal justification* or *justification from eternity*.

*   *   *

He who reflects seriously on justification through faith will do well to keep a sharp eye on the dangers that continually threaten his thought. He shall have to watch the horizons of faith's perspective for every intrusion upon the message of Scripture. This warning is particularly apropo at the moment, with divine election again the flaming center of theological discussion and the theologians occupied with the boundary separating the true Reformed and a speculative human conception of God's election. We must shake ourselves free from every deterministic and fatalistic theory and try to grasp the scriptural, and therewith religious, understanding of election. In spite of our sickly and witless attempts to give form to our thoughts on this matter, we understand intuitively that what we encounter in the Scriptures is not a speculative, metaphysical system proposed for our consent.

We are not discussing election here, it is true, but we do touch upon these questions when studying the relation between time and eternity in connection with justification by faith. This is quite apparent in Barth's extensive discussion of election. The most indicative point in his treatment is the insistence that the entire reality of God's purpose coincides with the revelation in Jesus Christ. The question of God's eternal resolution and justification in time as we have been considering it is eliminated from the discussion. Barth sees the "decree" as it is broached in Reformed theology as only a source of grief and misconstrual. The idea of an "absolute decree" is distasteful to him especially since it has been made, according to him, "the principle from which everything else is deduced."[17] In its

17. K. Barth, *Kirchliche Dogmatik*, II, 2, p. 86.

place he proposes that the doctrine of election be understood Christologically.[18] Supra- and infra-lapsarianism alike consider predestination as a static system resting in eternity.[19] Behind both lurks "the image of the absolute, the God who neither binds Himself nor is bound, and not the image of the Son of God who binds Himself and is thus bound in unity with the son of David." That is to say, neither supra- nor infra-lapsarianism works with the image of "God in Christ."[20] Barth protests against the "balanced" system of the Reformed doctrine of predestination, against the idolatry of the "absolute decree," and substitutes for these the "recognition of the elected man Jesus Christ as the sole object of divine predestination."[21]

Jesus Christ is, thus, the electing God and the elected man.[22] With this everything problematic in the relation between time and eternity is banished. By making Christ the object of predestination, Barth would lay a stable foundation under the Reformed teaching of Christ as the mirror of election.[23] It is clear that he is trying to protest against speculation by underscoring the historical reality of redemption, the reality that "Jesus Christ is the Word of God, perfect and incapable of being over-estimated." He allows for no "secret" election which could possibly relativize or lay open to question the revelation in Christ. It is Christ the mirror of redemption or, to use the Lutheran expression, the "book of life" over against every speculation as the basis for the assurance of salvation![24]

Barth is cognizant, of course, of the biblical passages which "directly and expressly speak of God's election or predestination," and, be they "not particularly numerous," we still have to "go back to them again and again and proceed from

18. *Ibid.*, p. 87.
19. *Ibid.*, p. 144.
20. *Ibid.*, p. 145.
21. *Ibid.*, p. 154.
22. *Ibid.*, p. 157.
23. *Ibid.*, p. 72.
24. *Ibid.*, p. 168.

there."[25] But he wants us to reflect that "the Word, presented in Scripture, who calls us, is the same Word of God who creates and reveals all knowledge of God and man and who as such is for all time perfect and incapable of being over-estimated, and from whom we may not allow ourselves to be separated by a single breath."[26] "The pre-temporal, eternal will of God is nothing other than the supra-temporal Eternal who has disclosed Himself as such and is active within time."[27] Hence, predestination can only be understood Christologically. "The reality of this eternal unity of God and man is a concrete decision. Its content has a name; it is a person. He is called, and is, Jesus Christ, and is for that reason not a *decretum absolutum.*"[28] The correlation between faith and revelation is a stranger in the sphere of the absolute decree. One cannot *believe* the absolute decree; he can only stare at it.

Barth presents us here with an extremely important question, a point which has troubled the best of minds ever since the Reformation. The correlation between faith and our salvation, as the reformers saw it, did not mean a correlation between faith and a secret election, but a correlation between faith and the salvation that is revealed to us and encounters us in Christ. The man who addresses himself to the hidden depths of God's purpose instead of to the historical revelation in Christ as it encounters us in the service of redemption has already run afoul of the truth. The reformers, no less than Barth certainly, willed every believer bound to Christ and every path that turned away from Him rejected as speculation. This was where their witness lay as to the ground of the assurance of salvation. The idea of Christ as the "mirror of election" becomes increasingly prominent as the antithesis between Christianity and determinism or fatalism becomes

25. *Ibid.,* p. 161.
26. *Ibid.,* p. 165; cf. p. 170.
27. *Ibid.,* p. 170.
28. *Ibid.,* p. 172. The "concrete decree" in the election of Jesus Christ must replace the "absolute decree." Cf. p. 173.

more sharply focused. For no such idea can be found in any form of determinism. This is of such great significance for the assurance of salvation that we can only accept this focus of the confession with profound gratitude. In it we share the deepest intent of the thought of both Luther and Calvin.

Calvinism has often been accused of having robbed the historical revelation of all its value and of setting every basic decision in the context of eternity. This criticism is particularly disturbing since, it were true, it would make of everything that is realized in time nothing but a medium of knowing what really occurred in eternity. And this would make of Christ only a teacher and a prophet of eternal truths. No actual decision could ever be made in time; nothing decisive could occur, neither in the cross or the resurrection. The confessions of the Reformed churches, however, are most articulate in their rejection of speculation; never did they proceed from an "eternal deduction" to strip the historical work of Christ of its divine and saving character. For this reason, Barth's doctrine of election ought to engage the serious attention of Reformed dogmatics.

This will call for an extensive discussion in the proper place, though even here one point is relevant. In Barth's teaching of Christ as the mirror of election, he makes divine election coincide with the election of Jesus Christ. Brunner has said that Barth's doctrine of Christ as the object of a double predestination[29] "is nowhere to be found in the Bible."[30] We may add that the consequences of his doctrine of election bring him continually to the precipice of *apokatastasis* or universalism. We must also question whether Barth really does justice to the depth of earnestness in the scriptural witness. It is quite fair to warn that God's purpose and His election "in Christ" must not be interpreted as a speculative-

29. *Ibid.*, p. 130.
30. E. Brunner, *Dogmatik*, I, p. 376.

idealistic system. For this would be to annul all assurance of salvation by canceling the reality of historical revelation. But neither must we historicize such terms. When the Scripture speaks to us of God's counsel, His eternal purpose, and His creative thinking it guides us into the depth of that which came to us *in* the Word of redemption. The mystery of the correlation between faith and revelation *realizes* itself within the boundaries of our temporal existence.

Though he reach far out beyond the horizons of his temporal circumstance, man never gets hold of Truth until he believes that Truth *came* in Jesus Christ. In the Word of Truth we encounter the mystery of His will as He has made it known to us: "Making known unto us the mystery of his will, according to his good pleasure which he purposed in him . . . in him, I say, in whom we also were made a heritage, having been foreordained according to the purpose of him who worketh all things after the counsel of his will" (Eph. 1:9-11). He who cuts himself off from *this* historical revelation, this *mensura humana,* historicizes both redemption and revelation, and cuts loose the eternal, divine perspective of grace from history. For, though we are set before the unsearchable judgment and untraceable ways of God and before the depths of the riches both of His wisdom and knowledge, we can perceive that in all these scriptural words the finger of the divine Word is pointed to the eternal "pre," the "from before" of God's love, which finds its pivot only in Christ irrespective of what we do or think. There is only one way for a man to travel, the way of faith in the inscrutable but traversable way which God has paved — the way of salvation that has no other goal than divine salvation.

The way of speculation by-passes the correlation of faith and grace. We shall, thus, give full vent to the totality of Scripture only if we subtract nothing from either the "beforehand" of

God's grace in Christ, or the promise of the gospel with which the living God has revealed Himself within our life.

*   *   *

In the entire gamut of theology, a pure insight of faith is of utmost importance for the relation between faith and justification. The preaching of salvation is perpetually threatened from two directions: on one hand from an over-estimation of the function of faith, by which the decisiveness of grace is made dependent upon human abilities and capacities, and, on the other hand, from a disruption of the correlation by making salvation so wholly objective that faith loses its decisive role in the correlation. The Church must avoid both Charybdis and Scylla. The jubilant song of assurance that we are justified by faith sounds through Holy Scripture — this is what Comrie meant to say by his "eternal justification." This idea becomes dangerous when we try to pursue it with logical consistency. If that is done, the reality of justification through faith is swallowed by rational speculation. However, the intent of the notion is not speculative, but religious. It was an attempt to give form to the pure content of *sola fide,* the disclaimer of every element of merit in faith as a human act, and therewith a rejection of the intrinsic value of faith. This is to say that it was a manner of expressing the depth of divine mercy and the mystery of His will which He has made known to us.

Sola fide is once and for all not a theoretical, one-sided construction. Its intent is to capitalize the Sovereign Grace in which faith finds its home. No dogmatic contemplation can rise above this. And dogmatics worth its salt does not want to, for it seeks no gnosis that is concealed to simple faith. Further than this it cannot go; more than this it cannot say. Dogmatic reflection, like simple faith, must honor God's order, the divine *way of salvation.* God's mercy comes to us in the administration of redemption along the trail of history. And in this we are guarded against speculation. For confronting us is the mirror of our election, Jesus Christ.

This was nicely expressed by Calvin: "In the first place, if we seek the fatherly clemency and propitious heart of God, our eyes must be directed to Christ, in whom alone the Father is well pleased . . . If we are chosen in him, we shall find no assurance of our election in ourselves; nor even in God the Father, considered alone, abstractly from the Son. Christ, therefore, is the mirror, in which it behooves us to contemplate our election; and here we may do it with safety."[31] Here is the antithesis to salvation through the *work* of faith as well as to any emasculation of the call to believe. In such a position we have the only durable resistance to any disruptive intrusion into the living correlation between faith and grace. Such intrusions usually purpose to cut off either one side of the correlation or the other, either human faith or divine grace. And to cut off one is to malign the other. For it is divine grace which is honored in faith as unmerited even by faith itself.

31. Calvin, *Institutes,* III, xxiv, 5.

The Value of Faith

CHAPTER VII

The Value of Faith

SINCE faith exists in correlation with justification, we must ask what the value of faith in that correlation is. If value is ascribed to faith in its correlation with grace, if faith is given an essential function to fulfill, and if faith is made imperative, is not justification ultimately dependent upon a human condition? Let all works of the law and merit be excluded, disclaim all reasons for self-flattery and self-righteousness, does not faith remain even then a human, creaturely *factor* to be reckoned with in a correct understanding of justification? Confess even that faith is a gift of God, is not *sola gratia* still threatened by the idea that faith has value?

* * *

The question of the value, the place and function of faith has been made more pertinent in recent years by the concept of faith in dialectical theology. When the dialectical theologians, in the early years of the movement, began to shout from the roofs about justification through faith alone, other thinkers were forced to consider anew the subjective side of the correlation. Human faith, as it were, looked us straight in the face and demanded that we account for it.

Was this faith the only way to God? Did all other ways lead only to idols? If morality, culture, and religion failed in their grand attempts to pierce the shroud of death which separates time from eternity and man from God, could human faith turn the trick? So, in the twenties, the problem of faith was one of the acute problems of theology, pushed upon us, so to speak, by the doctrine of justification. There was a magnificent effort to get above the subjectivism and psychologism that ruled the age into a sphere of objective faith. Brunner turned to Luther and found in him an anti-psychological theologian. He contends that Luther wanted to say "that justification through faith alone is that which God does, that which lies wholly beyond the human scope, not something that happens to or operates within the soul, not a spiritual dynamic, not an elevation of the inward life, nor any religious geniality of this earth; it is the total contradiction of all these. It is the denial of all human spirituality. It is the principial and radical disregard for all the processes of the inner man.[1] Faith has a transcendent character. It looks away from all human experience, "puts both feet on the other side of human experience."[2] There is a great gulf between faith and any human disposition. Faith is "pure objectivity" and disdains everything psychological. It is directed only to God, and the less one speaks of it the purer it is. It is the "empty form, which in and for itself is nothing, except as a vessel for its content."[3] Faith, Brunner goes on to say, is not a special form of ordinary human confidence, but a "primal-act," essentially different from every other act of confidence. It crosses over into the absolutely trans-subjective, is a negation of human activity.[4] Faith, he contends, falls outside the field of psychology; it is a leap into the beyond and is definable only by its object.[5]

Brunner underscores the "emptiness" of faith in order to bring out the positive side of its content. It is "the sacrifice of the soul to God, the lowering of the drawbridge to the divine invader who marches from the beyond into this earth and

---

1. E. Brunner, *Erlebnis, Erkenntnis und Glaube,* 1923, p. 35.
2. *Ibid.,* p. 37.
3. *Ibid.,* p. 92.
4. *Ibid.,* cf. pp. 92-96.
5. *Ibid.,* p. 101.

takes the lordship of the manor upon Himself."[6] Faith, he
goes on to say, is utter humility; it prostrates itself before the
divine miracle, the "wholly other." It is a break with everything psychological; it only listens and allows itself to be
judged.[7] Brunner sets all these statements in the framework
of his neo-Kantian viewpoint, but it is nevertheless clear that
he means thereby to express the truth of *sola fide-sola gratia*
and to discharge the subjective pole of the correlation faith-
grace of any active value.

Fredrich Gogarten draws the same curtain between faith
and the inner life. He insists that faith is not a neutral organ
that accepts divine revelation; it "belongs itself to revelation."[8]
It is not a function of "this side" which takes to itself "the
other side"; "it is itself something from the other side; it is a
miracle." Faith's place is, as seen with human eyes, empty.
It is nothing, it is only the border, the end of all human
possibility.[9] It is, continues Gogarten, not a "special organ,"
not "a human act which takes to itself the message of the forgiveness of sins."[10] Revelation lies on the opposite side of
all experience and, in its absolute objectivity, is "the death of
all experience and of everything temporal."[11]

This is somewhat how dialectical theology tried, in its early
days, to give an account of the way of faith. There was an
excessive emphasis on the idea that the way of faith is not a
trail blazed by man. The correlation was no longer human
subjectivity (faith) -divine objectivity (justification). There
was only a divine subjectivity, which revealed itself in the
justification of the ungodly. Nevertheless, we can say that
we are here faced with an attempt to formulate the Reformation

6. *Ibid.*
7. *Ibid., pp.* 127, 129, 131. Cf. Brunner, *Die Mystik und das Wort,* 1924,
pp. 79 f.
8. F. Gogarten, *Von Glauben und Offenbarung,* 1928, p. 48.
9. *Ibid.,* pp. 48-52.
10. *Ibid.,* p. 61.
11. F. Gogarten, *Die religiöse Entscheidung,* 1924, p. 59.

concept of faith as "mere instrument" and thereby to put the contrast between faith and human works on open display.

This is no less true of the theology of Karl Barth, who has also reflected much on the function and place of faith. In his thought, too, there is a forceful insistence on defining faith by its object. We need only recall the chapters in the *Römerbrief* in which faith is characterized as "miracle," "beginning," and "creation."[12] Faith is "never accomplished, never something at hand, never secure; it is, from a psychological viewpoint, a repeated leap into the unknown, into the darkness, into the empty air."[13] Everything human in faith is "unworthy of belief," and "if faith seeks to be more than a vacuum, it is unbelief."[14] Barth, in discussing Paul's phrase "justified through faith," says that the new man is the *subject* of faith. But who is this subject, this new man? "This subject is not I; in so far as it is a subject, in so far as it is what it is, namely absolutely objective, it is totally other and everything except what I am."[15]

Barth, too, is occupied with the emptiness of faith, not with the intent to disqualify faith, but to stress its connection with its object. Faith, he says, is "wholly and completely defined by what it believes."[16] Faith involves trust, *fiducia,* but then in the juridical sense, as acceptance of a deposit or confidence in a given word. The subject-object relationship is transposed — man is the object, God the Subject. Faith is not cast away; but it is, as it were, completely absorbed in the revelation and the faithfulness of God. Barth expresses this most radically when he contends[17] that faith is "not an act of man, but the

---

12. K. Barth, *Römerbrief,* Chap. IV.
13. *Ibid.,* p. 73.
14. *Ibid.,* p. 42.
15. *Ibid.,* p. 125.
16. K. Barth, *Prolegomena,* 1927, pp. 87 ff., particularly p. 89.
17. K. Barth, *Erklärung des Philipperbriefes,* 1928, p. 98.

original, divine believing." If we wish to say what faith is, then we must put all the emphasis upon its object. For faith has to do not with itself, but with *Christ*.

* * *

We should be doing this struggle with the nature of faith an injustice if we were to set it aside as a passing symptom of crisis thought. The dialectical theologians were often guilty of excessive statements which suggest that faith is a *donum superadditum*, a *donum novum* in God's hands, which remains external to concrete human existence. The greater care with which Barth formulated his views in later volumes of the *Dogmatik* suggests, too, that the expression of the earlier days of the twenties were fruits of reaction, to be regarded as tentative. Calvin, too, spoke of the emptiness of faith, saying that faith looks away from itself to Christ. This, too, offers a clue to the nature of faith. When Calvin talks of faith in this way, he is opposing himself to every possible righteousness that might arise from human condition or merit. He understood and formulated the correlation with utmost precision. Calvin does not disqualify faith in the correlation of faith and justification, but he does define faith in such a way that it lives and moves wholly from and in grace.[18] With this we encounter the question of what the Reformation meant by calling faith an *instrument*. This is the sixteenth century form of the problem which we face in our day anew as the contrast of the "emptiness" of faith to the meritoriousness of works. What did the

---

18. Cf. especially Calvin on Romans 3:27: "Sed Paulus ne guttam quidem reliquam facit. Deinde si per fidem tollitur operum gloratio, *ut non possit fides pure praedicari,* quim omnia Dei misericordiae deferendo prorsus hominem laude spoliet; sequitur nullis ad justitiam consequendam operibus nos adiuvari." P. Brunner in his *Glauben bei Calvin*, 1925, put a dialectical stamp on Calvin's idea of faith. Cf. especially pp. 35 ff. Brunner, however, read Calvin with dialectical lenses.

reformers really intend to say when they described faith as an instrument?

*   *   *

Lightly weighed, this ascription awakens some surprise; the thought of an instrument arbitrarily suggests something mechanical and some purposeful action by the one who has the instrument in his hands. And this is hardly congruent with the faith of the Reformation. How came it that this term was used by the reformers to translate something essential to the correlation between faith and justification? Can *faith as an instrument* convey the vital idea of a living, personal relationship of knowledge and trust in which the believer simply casts himself upon His Lord? Does the term *instrument* cover that which transports us into the mysterious work of the Holy Ghost, who Himself works in our hearts through the preaching of the gospel?

Of course, our feeble formulations can never adequately portray any portion of Christian truth. The question is whether the manner in which we ply these great concepts makes the teaching of Scripture clear. No one would be so rash as to claim that the ineffable mystery hidden in the word *faith* could be described by the term *instrument*. But we must try to find some term which would give at least an intimation of the relation of faith to justification. This is true of the use of the word in the Belgic Confession. This confession states that faith "is an instrument with which we embrace Christ our justification" (Art. 22). Immediately preceding this, it reads: "However, to speak more clearly, we do not mean that faith justifies us . . . *for* it is merely an instrument." This is not to say that faith has but slight significance. The Scriptures themselves cry out against a depreciation of faith: "Thy faith hath saved thee; go in peace" (Luke 7:50). "Daughter, be of good cheer; thy faith hath made thee whole" (Matt. 9:22) and "According to your faith be it done unto you" (Matt. 9:29). The Confession seeks to get at the nature of this same faith and tells us that God in Christ is our only true justification.

But our Lord, who attributes a miraculous healing to saving faith, also says, just as truly, of a similar miracle: "Go to thy house unto thy friends, and tell them how great things the Lord hath done for thee, and how he had mercy on thee" (Mark 5:19). Thus, we should not be surprised that the Canons of Dort, which were aimed so squarely at the Arminians, can speak, nevertheless of justifying faith (II, 8).

The description of faith as an instrument does not add a new element to *sola fide*; it only gives expression to this keynote of the Reformation. The Belgic Confession is in general agreement with Calvin's declaration that, "strictly speaking," it is God alone who justifies. Calvin aptly compares faith to an empty vessel, for "unless we come empty, with the mouth of our soul open, to implore the grace of Christ, we cannot receive Christ."[19] According to Calvin, too, faith is "only the instrument by which righteousness is received." Only thus, contends the reformer, can we crack the shell of the difficulty as to how faith must be understood.[20] We must come to Christ "empty," so that He alone may fill us with His grace. Faith justifies in the sense that "it receives and embraces the righteousness offered in the gospel."[21]

We receive the inheritance by faith, "and why is this, but because faith, without any assistance of works, depends wholly on the Divine mercy?"[22] Calvin proceeds, then, to say: "We are prepared, therefore, to seek and obtain the grace of God, discarding at the same time all confidence in ourselves, and relying solely on the assurance of His mercy . . ."[23] Nowhere does Calvin crystallize the mystery of the correlation more acutely than in this unique and paradoxical statement. He has

19. Calvin, *Institutes*, III, xi, 7.
20. *Ibid.*
21. *Ibid.*, 17.
22. *Ibid.*, 18.
23. *Ibid.*, xii, 8.

to torture human language in order to get at the mystery of
faith as it comes to reality through the Holy Ghost. In the
"preparedness" of which he speaks, we do not discover a hint
of meritorial function for faith. Therefore Calvin uses this
note repeatedly as a pastoral injunction, to make it clear "that
the heart is not open for the reception of his mercy unless it be
divested of all idea of its own dignity.[24] To supplement this
idea, he gropes for more lucid language, saying that faith "is a
thing merely passive, bringing nothing of our own to conciliate
the favour of God, but receiving what we need from Christ."[25]

The single connecting thread observable in all this is the
bond created by God to relate faith with His own mercy. We
have spoken often of a correlation in an attempt to suggest
the nature of this connection. The term is, naturally, open to
abuse; it could be construed as a relation in which both sides
are mutually dependent and reciprocally effective. This sense
destroys everything true about the relationship between faith
and justification. But the *correlation* of which we speak involves a relationship which is unique, *sui generis,* and which
therefore must remain ultimately mysterious. Negatively,
this much is clear about the mystery — the correlation is not
drawn about a subjective axis consisting of a work of love or
of obedience to God's commandments. Faith in the correlation
bespeaks the working of the Holy Spirit directing man to
God's grace. Thus understood, faith can never make God's
justifying act of grace relative; it is faith, true faith, which
honors the sovereignty of grace. And this is what the reformers and the confessions meant by speaking of faith as an
instrument, as well as by the emptiness, the vacuity, the pas-
sivity of faith. Such concepts in no way deny the activity of
faith, its grasp of its object, or its working itself out in love.
Faith is still a human act. The correlation between faith and
promise, faith and justification does not become a divine mono-

---

24. *Ibid.,* 7.
25. *Ibid.,* xiii, 5.

logue in which man is a mere telephone through which God addresses Himself. Sometimes in resistance to more subtle forms of work-righteousness, the phrase *divine faith* has been used instead of *human faith*. This was an attempt to avoid the tension of the subject-object relation as taught by the subjective theology of the nineteenth century and to break away from the construction of the correlation of faith and justification as a divine-human polarity. This reaction swung, in our century, to extremes (which, however, were often corrected later) in which the correlation became just such a divine monologue. The mystery of the correlation is apparent, however, only when it really embraces the reality of human existence.

The miracle of grace occurs in the act or attitude of faith, the faith that is roused by the Holy Spirit. With this, *sola gratia* is not spurned; it is verified. Grace does not mean an ontological cutting-off of a part of human life. The correlation is firmly rooted in concrete human existence; it is far from being sealed in the Godhead. But all pride is judged, everything which the human ego places high is thrown down. This is the meaning of *sola fide* as the unearned wealth of the gospel. This is the significance of faith, on which everything depends. Often faith is ascribed to the grace of God as being its creation side by side with other objects of the work of grace, without a further enquiry into the nature of this faith. In such incomplete teaching, faith as the gift of God is left undefended against subtle heresy. It may seem to assure the safety of the Church's confession and it may seem to honor the work of the Spirit; but the luster of the *sola fide* is not there, nor is the *sola* of the *gratia*.

*   *   *

Repentance is a boon companion of true faith; the man justified by faith is justified not as an innocent man, but as a guilty sinner, and, thus, repentance is also related to justification. Repentance has been subjected to the same abuse as has faith. The great leveling process in which faith and justification became two subjective or psychological poles of interdependence also affected repentance. This process had already insiduously endangered the Church during the first years of her existence; it came in under the guise of nomism, and finally celebrated its triumph in the medieval doctrine of penance. This kind of penance-nomism is a parasite on the true relation between repentance, sorrow, and grace.

This relation is taught in the Scriptures for all to read. We may recall Christ's biting remark about the healthy who need no aid (Matt. 9:12), the sinners called and given grace, the poor of spirit (Matt. 5:3), the weary and heavy laden whom He drew to Himself and saved (Matt. 11:28), and the humble, praying publican who went home justified (Luke 18:14). "Humble yourselves therefore under the mighty hand of God, that he may exalt you in due time" (I Pet. 5:6). Believers are urged to put on the garment of humility; for God resists the proud and gives grace to the humble (I Pet. 5:5). Mary sings her *Magnificat* and reveals the tremendous revolution that is under way: the mighty are displaced from their thrones, the proud are broken in the citadels of their hearts, the rich are turned away empty, while the hungry are filled and the humble exalted (Luke 1:51-53). It began, actually, in the Old Testament, as David witnesses: "The sacrifices of God are a broken spirit: A broken and a contrite heart, O God, thou wilt not despise" (Ps. 51:17).

Throughout the whole of Scripture the total humiliation in confession of guilt and sorrow for sin is portrayed as constitutional and essential in the religion of faith.

We realize, however, that the wholly scriptural connection between repentance and faith has often been interpreted in such a way as to destroy the simplicity of the gospel. Although the *apparent* intent was only to emphasize and describe this connection, this repentance actually became a preliminary condition which we must fulfill. In one way or another, *feeling*

sick was made a *condition* of the healing, and the human
activity, be it a negative one, of repentance was made a con-
stituent of salvation.

This began in the first centuries of the Church. In the
Second Letter of Clement there is a discourse on the making of
a counterpayment, that is, performing penance. Penance is
understood here as a payment which man offers to God, which
payment carries the guarantee of healing, for, the reasoning
goes, God knows beforehand what is in our hearts. We must,
of course, make much allowance for unhappy formulations,
but it is evident, even given such concession, that this was the
beginning of the development of the doctrine of penance which
later menaced the life of the Church and which made the
Reformation so imperative a crusade for the restoration of
the simplicity of the gospel. The power of healing and purification from sin had been dragged into the act of penance.
The psychological act of penance was in itself given healing
power.[26] From this we can readily understand how it came
that penitence was bound to various sorts of works of penance
such as alms and fasting, and how the biblical relationship
between penitence and faith was threatened with extinction.

The correlation between repentance and grace was re-
fashioned into a causal relation, in which the act of penitence
and the works of penance were given a causal connection
with divine grace. It was still possible to acknowledge scriptural passages in which the correlation was taught, but the
estrangement from the message of unmerited grace had already
occurred. It was impossible to see any longer that penitence
was opposed to the earning of grace by penance. The parallel

---

26. There is a striking parallel to this in Max Scheeler, then a Roman
Catholic philosopher of religion, when he wrote "Reue und Wiedergeburt"
in *Vom Ewigen im Menschen*, I, 1923. Cf. "On the contrary, penance, as
purely moral, is a form of the soul's self salvation" (p. 12); "Penance
truly destroys every psychical quality that we can call guilt" (p. 41); and,
"Penance is the mighty force of self-regeneration in the moral realm. . . ."
(*Ibid.*). Such notions of "guilt" could appear only in the Roman world
of thought on penance.

between this and the question of the nature of faith is self-evident. As *sola fide* was smirched by a meritorial idea of faith, so the true nature of penitence was corrupted into an obligatory human pre-requisite. It is profoundly significant that when the Reformation proclaimed *sola fide,* it was attacking the Roman doctrine of penance. To the superficial reader, this antithesis was denied in Luther's statement that "only humility saves," but a closer look reveals how deeply this *humilitas* was entrenched in the Reformation.[27] For this humility is one with faith, confronting and opposing every earned merit. The Reformation lives or dies with the contrast between *humilitas* and *superbia,* between penitence and the works of supererogation. Only against this background is it possible to say that humility saves, even as it was once said: "Thy faith hath made thee whole."

In the struggle with Rome the Reformation sensed intuitively that, in spite of her accent on prevenient grace, Rome had turned the relation between penitence and grace into a legalistic conditional stipulation. It is no wonder that when this legal bond between human condition and grace was broken the foundation of our salvation again came in sight.

*　　*　　*

Calvin, too, occupied himself with the question of penitence and the gospel. He declares that the Roman sophists taught a doctrine of penitence that raises the question "by what means, by what law, on what condition, and with what facility or difficulty, remission of sins may be obtained."[28] But the ques-

---

27. Luther's first thesis reads: "Dominus et magister noster Jesus Christus docendo: Penitentiam agite etc. omnem vitam fidelium penitentiam esse voluit." Christ wills that the entire life of the faithful be a life of penitence. Dillschneider says correctly that the Reformation meant "the restoration of the original biblical perspective" through which the sacrament of penance was uprooted and penitance was again made relevant to the whole life. Cf. O. Dillschneider, *Evangelische Offenbarung, Die Grundlage der evangelische Theologie,* 1939, p. 179.
28. Calvin, *Institutes,* III, iv, 2.

tion is a treacherous one, for if forgiveness waits upon the fulfillment of a human condition, said Calvin, it leaves us in the most wretched of all possible positions. Calvin opposes the notion that the degree of penitence must be in proportion to the greatness of guilt. To put a man's inner life in the scale, weighing his anguish against his confidence of pardon, is to drive the soul to despair. Calvin admits the relation between repentance and forgiveness, but insists that the penitence is not the cause of the forgiveness.[29] To isolate the soul's remorse and make it a factor in its own right is to focus all the interest of the remorseful on his own contrition. Calvin says to the contrary that the sinner ought "not to look on his compunction or on his tears, but to fix his eyes solely on the mercy of God."[30]

It should be clear now what the issues of the struggle regarding the doctrine of penance were. Basically, the same things were at stake as in the dispute about *sola fide*. The Reformed confessions recognize a profound connection between the gospel and the poor of spirit, healing and sickness, comfort and mourning, rest and weariness; but they rule out any nominalistic deformation of this connection. Faith does not place a man before a certain number of accepted truths which he intellectually assents to; faith thrusts him, as a sinner, before God's holiness. He does not try to escape judgment by means of faith; in faith he accepts the justness of the judgment. Thus, faith is bound inseparably to repentance; and meritorial worth is ostracized as much from the realm of penitence as from that of faith.

This is the background of Calvin's view of penitence and faith. It has been pointed out by others that Calvin also recognized a repentance (*poenitentia*) which precedes faith, but that this was gradually driven to the background as he

29. *Ibid.*, 3.
30. *Ibid.*

increasingly emphasized the repentance which flows from faith and has its place *within* the Christian life.[31] Already in 1536, Calvin was not prepared to deny that terrors of conscience before God might occur previous to actual faith and conversion. For he was unwilling to press God's manner of leading man to salvation into a definite system. He saw true penitence as a concomitant of faith, of true faith which does not deny its demerits in the face of judgment but grasps grace from the hand of Him who received God's judgment in our stead.[32] Proceding from this point, Calvin offers, in the same year 1536, a thorough-going argument against the sacrament of penance.[33] The single point at issue was *the forgiveness of sins.*

The believer receives forgiveness, Calvin says, in the way of penitence. The phrase *in the way of* is the customary Reformation response to any idea of meritorial penance, as it is to any misformation of the faith-justification relationship. It is doubtful whether a dogmatic definition could ever be more clear than this, for in this we see the mystery of the correlation between penitence and divine grace. They are inseparable, but never interdependent. Repentance is necessary to the correlation, but it never earns or merits grace. Grace is given *in the way of* penitence, but it is always independent and undeserved.

It may seem that the phrase *in the way of penitent faith* only adds another tautology to a theological discussion and says nothing enlightening about the *way* of salvation. Against the background of various misconstructions of the correlation, however, it is this "tautology" which gives us a pure insight just because it maintains the mystery. This was what the fathers of Dort had in mind when they confessed concerning the falling away of believers that they "interrupt the exercise of faith . . . until, when they change their course by serious

---

31. Cf. H. Bavinck, *Gereformeerde Dogmatiek,* III, pp. 521 ff.
32. Calvin, *Institutes,* III, ii, 1.
33. Calvin, *Opera Selecta* (ed. Niesel), I, pp. 172 ff.

repentance, the light of God's fatherly countenance again shines upon them" (V, 4).

Thus, the singularity of this *way* becomes more apparent. Calvin comments on this singularity in the context of his treatment of faith.[34] It is not subject to systematization; it can be understood only by faith. Dogmatic exposition cannot rationalize it into an easier way on which to walk. It can only warn against the danger, so serious in the light of history, that "conditionalism" makes itself master of the correlation. It can, besides, lead us to the scriptural singularity of penitent faith which, in its very nature, can know nothing but God's mercy.

* * *

All this gives us no occasion to gloss over one word of what Scripture teaches of the *necessity* of faith. With this statement, we strike, for the last time, the central point of our study. We must not allow ourselves, in reaction to the doctrine of faith's meritoriousness, to become too timid to speak of its necessity. This is a very real hazard. It would be possible for us, upon consideration of *sola gratia* in its truly exclusive and radical sense, to conclude that an insistence on the singular necessity of faith tends to relativize grace. The Holy Scriptures point with weighted decisiveness to this necessity. This is, of course, not a legalistic caveat, but it is an urgent call to faith. There is a continuous press toward the way of faith. Let it be written in capitals, put in italics that salvation is God's salvation, coming to us in the miracle of redemption, God's salvation which has been devised by no human mind and has risen from no human heart. None of this changes a letter of the fact that this sovereign grace *must* be accepted in faith.

The way that Scripture speaks of faith permits us to ascribe value to faith. This value comes in exhortation and warning.

---

34. *Institutes,* III, ii, 1.

Fear not! Only believe! The scriptural message of the necessity of faith can be summarized with the words of our Lord: "He that believeth and is baptized shall be saved, but he that disbelieveth shall be condemned" (Mark 16:16). Decision must be made, decision of frightening consequence. The Scripture rarely speaks of salvation without mentioning this urgency of belief. Psalm 27 leaves us in no uncertainty as to the origin and the objectivity of the salvation of which it sings. The poet knows about the sovereignty of grace. Jehovah is my light and my salvation, he says. But hear him further: ". . . unless I had *believed* to see the goodness of Jehovah" (Ps. 27:13).

The same urgency is apparent in warnings to the unbeliever. The children of Israel harden their hearts and refuse to hear the prophets, as their fathers refused to believe the Lord their God (II Kings 17:14). The divine wrath they incur is provoked by their unbelief (II Kings 17:18). Fire is ignited against Jacob and His wrath flames against Israel "because they believed not in God" (Ps. 78:22). Again, "If ye will not believe, surely ye shall not be established" (Is. 7:9). Israel's unbelief is compared with God's gifts: "For all this they sinned still, and believed not in his wondrous works" (Ps. 78:32). *"Therefore* their days did he consume in vanity" and their years in terror" (Ps. 78:33).

Everything would seem to wait upon faith. Comfort and warning find each other in Christ's statement: "He that believeth on the Son hath eternal life; but he that obeyeth not the Son shall not see life, but the wrath of God abideth on him" (John 3:36). This condition has such evident power that Paul, who knew nothing but Christ and Him crucified, writes that it pleased God to save *those who believe* through the foolishness of preaching (I Cor. 1:21; cf. John 20:27-29).

* * *

Scripture also underscores the value of faith by showing its power. The lives of the partiarchs are characterized as lived in and through faith. And life in faith is surrounded by wondrous things; through faith kingdoms are conquered, mouths of lions are shut, justice prevails, the fiery flames refuse to consume. The results of faith extend to the very border of life and death. Women have their dead restored and through faith martyrs refuse the offer of escape (Heb. 11:33 ff).[35]

The teaching of Christ was particularly clear about the power of faith. That the disciples were powerless to cast out a demon from the lunatic boy was due to their unbelief. And Christ said to them, "For verily I say unto you, If ye have faith as a grain of mustard seed, ye shall say unto this mountain, Remove hence to yonder place; and it shall remove; and nothing shall be impossible unto you" (Matt. 17:20). This faith does not know the impossible. We are told that all things are possible not only for God, but also for those who believe (Mark 9:23). The word possible is the translation of the Greek *dunamis* in which lies "the basic notion of capability, the ability given on basis of capacity."[36] What sort of "possibility," what kind of *dunamis* is this, that John can speak of it as overcoming the world (I John 5:4)? What is this power that destroys the power of unbelief and what is it that it can be frustrated by unbelief too, as Jesus testifies when He says that He could not exercise His *dunamis* because of unbelief (Mark 6:6)? And does it not strike us as strange that Christ should ask, "Nevertheless, when the Son of man cometh, shall he find faith on the earth?" (Luke 18:8), and that he should pray for Peter that his faith not fail him (Luke 22:32)?

Does not all this speak to us of the peculiar value of faith, indeed, of its decisiveness? Is there any fault to find with one who preaches and teaches this imperative with unusual stress? Can such a stress conform with the exclusiveness of

---

35. The word faith in Hebrews has its own color, and may not *per se* be identified with Paul's use of the word. On the other hand, it is never for a moment to be considered apart from faith in God's sovereign grace.

36. Kittel, *Theologisches Wörterbuch zum N. T.*, II, pp. 286 f.

sola gratia? And is the power of faith in harmony with the fact that it is God with whom all things are possible?

Such questions are made no less urgent by various scriptural qualifications to faith. There is the *great* faith of the Canaanite woman, that woman who desired the cure of her daughter so much that she was willing, as a foreigner, to eat the scraps off the table, and to whom Christ said: "O woman, thy faith is great. Be it so unto you as thou wilt" (Matt. 15:28). There is the great faith of the centurion from Capernaum, so great, that our Lord found none such in all of Israel (Matt. 8:9 ff.). As Jesus marveled at the stature of this faith, so He marveled at the unbelief of His own disciples. Recall how He chided them for their little faith, worrying as they were about clothing and provisions (Matt. 6:30) or trembling at their oars in the storm (Matt. 8:26). Scripture presents faith to us in its power and dynamic force, its firmness (Col. 2:5), its preciousness (II Pet. 1:1), and — as a climax — as the "most holy faith," upon which believers are told to build (Jude 20).

*   *   *

On the basis of these and many other similar declarations in Scripture, we may be inclined to imagine that Lord's Day 23 of the Heidelberg Catechism, which tells us that we cannot please God with the worthiness of our faith, conflicts with the power, the possibility, the preciousness, and the great value of this faith. In the flood of such scriptural ascriptions, the uniqueness of the correlation between grace and faith becomes particularly apparent. To interpret faith as a condition that comes along with salvation to supplement and complete it would be to manipulate faith into a kind, though a peculiar kind, of work of the law. And this would touch the sovereignty of grace. The marvelous fact is this, that *the way of salvation is the way of faith just because it is only in faith that the exclusiveness of divine grace is recognized*

and honored. This is not perspicuous to the reason, but it is
to him who takes hold of divine grace in the act of faith.
As penitence excludes all merit, so too faith, directed only to
divine mercy, excludes all worthiness. Paradoxical though
it may be, it is in this exclusion of worthiness that the worth
of true faith is brought out.

It is only thus that every scriptural discourse about faith
can be understood. For this is the only way of discovering
the relations in which faith stands. The potency of faith
(everything is possible to those who believe) is not an autonomous power side by side with the power of God; it exists only
because faith is completely directed to the power and blessing
of God. Faith is no competitor of *sola gratia;* but sovereign
grace is confirmed by faith. Only rationalism can make an
unevangelical condition out of this correlation, a *conditio sine
qua non,* a cooperating cause, a defining factor of salvation.
This rationalism can be broken through only in the act of
faith, in the act of penitent faith which knows that it is no
supplement to grace and which in this knowledge, praises
God's absolutely and completely *free* grace.

The biblical message of the necessity of faith is concerned
with this true faith. Its necessity is entrenched in *sola gratia.*
For faith moves completely in Jesus Christ, in *His* grace, *His*
power, *His* capability, *His* holy command. Great faith is revealed in the humility of the Canaanite woman and in the stubborn confidence of the centurion. This faith lacks all self-
worthiness and for this reason can be typified by its steadiness
and by its utter holiness — descriptions which can be applied
as well to the penitence shown in faith as to faith itself.

It should not pass unnoticed that Jude speaks of the high
holiness of faith just in order to exclude any merit from it.
For this faith keeps a man in the love of God and praying
in the Holy Ghost "looking for the mercy of our Lord Jesus
Christ unto eternal life" (Jude 21). It is telling that Jude's let-

ter ends with a paean to the glory of God in Christ Jesus (Jude 24, 25). There is no tension, there is only profound accord between the glory of God and the noble holiness of faith.

*   *   *

Faith is always a divine gift, always a work of the Holy Spirit; and it is even so within this correlation. Faith is not conceived by flesh and blood. The womb of our heart is barren. Our hearts, by nature, preferably prevent conception, and the history of heresy is evidence of how easily our treacherous hearts arise to the occasion. "For by grace have ye been saved through faith; and that not of yourselves, it is the gift of God" (Eph. 2:8). There are sound arguments that the words "it is the gift of God" refer to faith. If this be so — though *sola gratia* does not get its breath from the exegesis of a single text — the correlation between faith and grace is underwritten here with remarkable clarity and expressness. Only through the most absurd obstinacy could anyone escape the fact that this text rejects quite finally even the most refined doctrine of conditional merit.

This divine gift is without strings. There is nothing in man that could possibly succeed as a condition. Nor is saving faith a particular form of general human faith; "faith in God" and "faith in my friend" are not two species of the same genus. The difference between faiths does not exist only in their having different objects. This would destroy the uniqueness of true faith, which is not a general confidence directed, in this case to God. Faith itself is defined by its object, defined and determined as to its totality and root. The act of faith is as much being held by God as holding Him; the power of faith is exercised as much in capitulation as in conquering — the faith that overcomes the world is capitulation to Christ's great victory. This faith is truly a gift, a gift which is totally unique because of its object and which in that uniqueness can lead us on the way of salvation. Beware least anyone sap this tree!

On the other hand, this faith is not a gift in the sense of a *donum superadditum* added to human nature as a new organ. This would mean that an unbeliever is less of a human than a believer. Such a notion is the result of cutting off faith from total concreteness of human life. It may seem to honor the miracle of this gift the more, but actually it does injustice to the gift itself. Faith is neither a newly created human organ nor a new substance which is infused into the level of human existence. If it were, it would be scarcely distinguishable from the Roman *donum superadditum*. We cannot get at grace by compiling a studied list of anthropological data. The whole man beginning at his heart, from which are the issues of life, is embraced by this immutable and miraculous divine grace. This is the miracle of the Spirit that remains indescribable although the attempts to describe and define it are legion. Instead of calling faith a new organ or a *donum superadditum,* the work of the Holy Spirit has been described as the great change of course from the way of apostasy to the way of the true God. Such a description surely has its value. It seeks to maintain the *donum purum* over against the *donum superadditum.* But its value is kept only when it is not forgotten that the direction, structure, and content of faith may never be set loose from one another. Faith is not a change of direction within a general subjective area already existent, an area in which faith is one function along with the acts of so-called faith that are present in most human relationships. For the change of direction involved in true faith includes faith's content. In the sphere of general or common human faith and fidelity, faith is a condition in the full and ordinary sense of the word. The faith which is God's saving gift, however, is defined by its content and, this being God's sovereign work in Christ, excludes faith as a condition. All this is necessary to the correlation of faith and grace and this, in its recognition of *sola gratia,* defines the nature of the correlation.

*   *   *

Perhaps the most typical of the scriptural passages relevant to our present study is the familiar text of Hebrews 11:6: "And without faith it is impossible to be well-pleasing unto him." It is not difficult to understand how a man bothered with the doctrine of faith as a human condition of salvation would be attracted to this text and led thereby to assign to faith a subjective "quality" that God finds to His satisfaction. And we should ask ourselves honestly whether, with this text before us, we can still maintain that we are *not* well-pleasing to God because of our faith. For this is what the Catechism teaches.[37] Furthermore, what is the connection between this capacity to please and our precious *sola gratia?*

These questions open up our whole problem anew. The text would seem to allow only one interpretation. Must we not go along with the exposition that "a common article in the biblical doctrine of salvation is that faith is a condition for divine approval and inexpendable for fellowship with God; it accepts two truths: the existence of God and the divine endorsement of the God-seeker."[38] Actually we get little from this, since the word *condition* is used without further explication. As in most considerations of Hebrews 11:6, we find in Windisch only a brief exegesis, which does not deal extensively enough with the unique relationship that is suggested here between faith and the good pleasure of God.

The word *impossible* is accented in the text: Impossible that man should please God without faith! It has been pointed out that four impossibilities, marking the boundaries of the realm of salvation, are recorded in the book of Hebrews: (1) that anyone once enlightened and thereupon fallen away be

---

37. Heidelberg Catechism, Lord's Day 23.
38. H. Windisch, *Der Hebräerbrief* in *Handbuch zum N. T.,* 1931, p. 100.

renewed (Heb. 6:4), (2) that God should lie (Heb. 6:18), (3) that the blood of bulls or goats should take away sins (Heb. 10:4), and (4) that man should please God without faith. These "impossibilities" vary much in nature and grounds. The first impossibility (renewal after falling away) suggests a limit to the work of the Holy Spirit and the powers of the coming age. The second (that God should lie) relates to the fidelity of God, which was underscored by the swearing of an oath, so that the heirs of His promise would see more clearly "the immutability of his counsel," i.e., the impossibility of His being false. The third is the impossibility of any purifying power in animal blood, another recollection of the continually repeated sacrificial rites of old Israel.

Then follows the fourth impossibility which touches upon the correlation between human faith and divine grace. Its reference to faith is negative, but one can read in it a positive connection between faith and the divine approval. The text is set in a context which is concerned with that strange Old Testament figure, Enoch. "By faith Enoch was translated that he should not see death; and he was not found, because God translated him: for he hath had witness borne to him that before his translation he had been well-pleasing unto God" (Heb. 11:5). Against this historical reference to a man who pleased God by faith, comes the statement that without faith it is impossible to please Him. The relation between faith and God's pleasure was illustrated in Enoch's life. All we know of the original story is what we find in Genesis 5:22, which tells us that Enoch walked with God and that God took him, living, to Himself. This walk is presented by the author of Hebrews as a walk of faith. Enoch pleased God, and God took him to Himself so that he did not have to pass through death. The text of Hebrews is a bit more extensive than the Genesis account, though the Greek version of Genesis adds that Enoch pleased God. Hebrews at any rate concludes that Enoch's walk in faith pleased God and that we may therefore say that he was transported through his faith. Enoch, living in a wicked environment, stayed by the side of God, walked with Him in faith, and this pleased God. *And without* faith it is impossible to please Him.

With Enoch's walk with God in mind, we cannot conclude that Hebrews 11:6 ascribes a meritorial worth to faith. It is not as though Enoch possessed a certain moral quality that God approved of. It was his whole existence, totally determined by his walk with God, that was involved. He was with God; and this has nothing to do with any accomplishment in the works of the law. It was in this faith, in this walk with God, that Enoch pleased Him. Without this faith, we cannot please God.

Again we are faced with the complete antithesis between faith and work-righteousness. The book of Hebrews does not work out this idea in discursive form. The purpose of the author is another one than that of Paul, though the two are not mutually exclusive. He is occupied with perseverance in faith, in the faith which directs itself continually to God and therein reveals its power. All that he says, with all his nuances, is in complete accord with what the Scriptures say elsewhere of the worth of faith. He does not invest man with an independent quality of worthiness, but with a faith which is colored and qualified by a walk with God. The phrase "with God" is what settles everything. It prevents us from construing from Hebrews 11:6 or any other passage of Scripture a doctrine of merit or achievement.

If we do not see this we are in no position to contend against Rome, against Osiander's sympathizers, or against Arminianism. For the mystery of faith must mean that man looks away from himself, and perseveres in his movement toward and walk with God. This is the faith that pleases God. Hebrews 11:6 establishes this firmly; it teaches, in its own right, the pure correlation of faith and sovereign grace.

We can, therefore, speak of the necessity of faith. This is also why unbelief is so sharply rebuked in the gospel and why Christ promises that the Comforter will come to "convict the world in respect of sin . . . because they believe not on me" (John 16:8, 9). Scripture, then, establishes the necessity of faith, and that without giving us a shred of argument for ascribing merit to faith itself. The gospel calls men urgently to faith, to believing acceptance of salvation, to the obedience of faith.

The obedience of faith — this is another expression which gives us a hint as to the nature of faith. It too may seem, at first sight, to water down our *sola gratia*. For obedience is a correlative of law. Does it not put the stamp of legalism on faith and betray it as a new work of the old law? The obedience of faith, however, does not involve subjugation to a general law. It is not susceptible to characterization according to its formal structure as a dutiful subjection. This obedience and subjection cannot be abstracted from Him to whom the believer subjects himself. We cannot close our eyes to the element of obedience in faith, but if we see it aright we shall realize that it serves to show us how completely faith is directed to its object. Recall Paul's description of total subjection as imprisonment; the man who is obedient in faith subjects all reasoning and every consideration in servitude to Christ.

Obedience is essential to faith for it illustrates the truth that faith is not autonomous and self-sufficient — that it capitulates in total surrender. Faith is not one modal manifestation of a basic concept called obedience in the same sense as that there are different ways in which we are subject to a certain basic law. Faith is the basic concept which is further described and characterized by the expression *obedience of faith*. That obedience of faith is consistent with *sola gratia* is illustrated by the way that Paul speaks of preaching and the sending of preachers in Romans 10. "And how shall they preach, except they be sent? Even as it is written, How beautiful are the feet of them that bring glad tidings of good things! But they did not all hearken to the glad tidings" (Rom. 10:15, 16). The older version has the last sentence thus: "But they did not all obey the gospel." There is no real difference between the older and newer versions. The kind of hearing meant in one is the same as the kind of obeying meant in the other. To hear the gospel is to obey it. Not to hear is to disobey it. And to believe is the same as to hear and obey, even as disbelieving is not hearing and not obeying. The obedience of faith, then, is really just faith — the total response to the gospel (cf. Rom. 16:26; Acts 6:7). Of this, again, Abraham, the father of believers, is the classic example.

*　　*　　*

Finally, the urgency of preaching is underscored by the scriptural witness to the necessity of faith. It is not inconceivable that the sovereignty of grace be taken as an occasion to soften the bitter earnestness of preaching. What human decision can have real significance, it could be argued, given the all decisive divine act of redemption? It could be proposed as an ultimate antithesis to Arminianism, or to any attempt to make faith an autonomous human act, that how man reacts to the divine decision is relatively insignificant. But this would be to dilute faith out of dread that its great strength render the decisiveness of divine grace ineffectual. The alertness to any threat to sovereign grace, from which this sort of reasoning arises, is, of course, commendable by Reformation standards. The trouble with it is that it reasons from a given concept of *sola gratia* to a position that can really give no quarter to the urgency of faith as Scripture presents it.

The problem here suggested is best seen if we glance at Barth's conception of the relation between election and faith (and unbelief). Barth is occupied all through his dogmatics with faith and revelation. It is to preserve the relation between faith and revelation that he throws out the idea of an "absolute decree," which, he says, no man can believe. In its place comes his "concrete decree" as seen in the reprobation and election of Jesus Christ. This is not an eternal decree, but a decree given in time. Given the reprobation of Christ, unbelief becomes a denial of the undeniable fact that only Jesus Christ is rejected by God. "That man is reprobate who isolates himself from God in denying that he is really elect in Jesus Christ. God is gracious to him; he is not thankful to God. God accepts him; he refuses God. God forgives him his sins; he holds on to them as though they were not forgiven."[39] This surely forces the issue as to the nature of the correlation between faith and election. On one hand, there is at this decisive point a similarity to universalism which pictures the relation between divine salvation and man as that of two concentric circles — the larger, universal salvation, and the smaller within it, man. All men are enclosed in the circle of universal salvation; man's disbelief of it does not alter the fact. What is remarkable in Barth is that according to him man is unable to get out of the sphere of grace; man's deed cannot undo that of God. "They can bring disgrace to divine election; they cannot annul or cancel it."[40] The dubious efforts of unbelief to disbelieve in its own election are impotent — "powerless against the will and decision of God." Unbelievers, then, can only be "potentially reprobate." Once the sword of wrath has been wielded, the unbeliever cannot put hands on it to use it against himself. It has struck down the Lord of Glory; it cannot strike a second time, try as the unbeliever may to deserve its blow. This is how Barth seeks to arrive at the relation between faith and grace. He does

---

39. K. Barth, *Kirchliche Dogmatik*, II, 2, p. 498.
40. *Ibid.*, p. 385.

not wish to be counted a universalist and he wants, in spite
of his doctrine of election in Christ, to put a certain "decision"
of faith in the hands of man.   He recalls unbelief's futile
effort to annul God's gracious decision of grace and calls it
"highly dangerous" — a matter of life and death.   It is impossible, however, to see why unbelief should be so dangerous
if the divine decision cannot be undone nor the sword of wrath
strike twice.   Yet Barth refuses to reason consistently from
the decisiveness of divine grace.   He is curbed by his consciousness of the "crisis of faith" and, in spite of his previous
thoughts, manages to ascribe a certain significance to faith.

What Barth finally concludes about the correlation is not
clear from his doctrine of election.   On one side, he sees the
reprobate as standing within the area of election, and on the
other, he tries to give weight to the seriousness of unbelief.[41]
Brunner calls the idea that the unbeliever is elect in Christ
a "fundamental deformation of the Christian gospel of salvation."[42]   Brunner criticizes Barth's concept as "objectivism,"
and perceives, correctly, that it involves an understanding of
the relationship between faith and revelation.   What he dis-
likes in Barth's "objectivism" is that "the subjective element,
faith, stands on a lower rung than, and is far subordinate to,
revelation, the objective Word of God."   Brunner would rather
put faith and revelation on the same level.   But no matter
how much it accentuates the significance of faith, we may
never put faith on the same rung with divine revelation.
Brunner's formulation is surely unfortunate, as is seen again
when he says that the effect of Barth's view is to find the
"real decision only in the objective, rather than in the subjective realm."[43]   Yet he has undeniably pointed out a vacuum

---

41. *Ibid.*, p. 552.
42. Brunner, *Dogmatik*, I, p. 377.
43. *Ibid.*, p. 379.

in Barth's doctrine of election, a vacuum that comes clearly to light in his easy-going attitude toward *unbelief*.[44]

There is really no excuse for taking the edge off the seriousness of unbelief. The Scriptures, in their proclamation of salvation, allow us no other alternative than to see unbelief in its most disastrous proportions. They preach the necessity of faith, and do it with an urgency which is existential to the core. This is evident throughout them. They do not offer us a note of information; they come with an importunate message demanding an answer of faith. The insoluble relation offers the only possibility of preaching the sovereignty of grace and the earnestness of the call to faith. Here lies the real mystery of the way of salvation.

---

44. The references above are to Barth's teaching in 1942. It is interesting to compare this with his earlier ideas. In his *Credo* of 1935, he stressed the decisive character of faith more strongly. At the same time, nevertheless, he accented the unconditional character of grace as much as he was to do in 1942. He writes, for instance, in *Credo*: "The power of Christian preaching and the force of Christian dogmatics stands or falls with this, that it sees man as in Christ, that it views him as belonging to God, that it therefore cannot count on his perseverance in unbelief or on his being eternally lost. The gospel declares an unconditional pardon, and the law is only active when it gets its voice from the gospel" (K. Barth, *De apostolische Geloofsbelijdenis*, 1935, p. 209). That he desires to maintain the urgency of faith becomes clear for he follows this immediately by saying that the declared truth of dogmatics must not include a denial of the possibility that man may be hardened and eternally lost. For this would take away the force of the Credo as the presupposition of the Christian confession. The *Credo* involves a decision: "it must be earnestly and urgently asked, 'Do you *believe* this?'." In 1935, then, we see the same two separate lines that appear in the *Kirchliche Dogmatik*. Cf. also his *Die Botschaft von der freien Gnade Gottes*, 1947, in which the unconditionalness of grace is thus expressed: "God's grace encounters man; to be man means to be encountered by God's grace. Jesus Christ would not be the Word through whom all things are created, if we could withdraw from this objective, this ontological reality to which all our decisions can be referred" (p. 6). But here, too, he shies away from universalism, for, as he says, a grace which automatically includes everyone would not be truly *free* grace: "God calls us in the decision of faith." In spite of this, it is clear that he out-Remonstrants the Remonstrants and exceeds the teaching which is rejected in the Canons of Dort, "that the purpose of the death of Christ [was] . . . only that He should acquire for the Father the mere right to establish with man such a covenant as He might please" (II, Rejection of errors, 2).

We could not speak of a mystery, if faith were made autonomous and were thus given a value in itself — if faith were its own validation. Let this be done and we shall have made of the relation a working partnership in which both parties, faith and grace, are of equal standing. This would spoil the essential correlation between faith and grace. The mystery of the way of salvation exists in the call to the faith which expects everything and rests its all in divine grace. Herein lies the seriousness of the decision of faith, of the necessity of a choice to which Scripture continually witnesses. The Scriptures preach the call to a faith which recognizes the exclusive divine character of grace.

This profound relationship can be understood only in faith. Apart from it we shall only construct another apparently logical, but essentially speculative system in which salvation arises from two cooperative factors or in which faith and disbelief are not taken in their deep seriousness. In both events, the mystery of God's way of salvation is abandoned. To avoid this, we are obliged in our preaching and in our reflection to affirm the identity of *sola fide* and *sola gratia*. Only thus can we send out the call to believe without doing injustice to the sovereignty of grace. For divine salvation is preached *in* the urgent appeal. Faith is fulfilled in this salvation. Only in faith can we transcend the entanglement which has so often dimmed the light of divine salvation in the history of the Church.

*   *   *

Sola gratia and *sola fide,* thus, remain the be all and end all of the relation between faith and justification. But we do not set up a technique; we are not concerned to defend a verbal talisman. For this too can become a bromide. It guarantees nothing by its incantation. There is no *a priori* surety against the errors and confusion which menace and confine our understanding of divine salvation. Our formulation surely provides none. Furthermore, we are not justified through sound theology; faith alone saves us.

But let the sound of *sola fide-sola gratia* ring in the life of the Church. Let it be a warning against the pride of the treacherous heart. Let it warn us all lest we take our lives in our own hands and so deny the Lord.

The confession of *sola fide-sola gratia* leads us along a dangerous road. There are traps and pitfalls along the way. Believers, too, can be victims. For if we misread the signs, our lives are confounded and the process of holiness is endangered. *Sola fide-sola gratia* is not a threat; it helps us to find the true way. It leads us into the right relation between faith and sanctification. We are on the way; there is no stopping and no return. As *sola fide-sola gratia* has established the relationship between "faith and justification," it must guide us through "faith and sanctification." All of which is to paraphrase the words of Paul: "What shall we say then? Shall we continue in sin, that grace may abound? God forbid. We who died to sin, how shall we any longer live therein?" (Rom. 6:1, 2).

Index of Persons and Subjects

Index of Texts

205

Printed in the United States
15559LVS00005B/34-42